I SPEAK,

THEREFORE

I AM

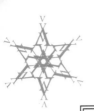

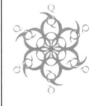

I SPEAK,
THEREFORE I AM

---

*Seventeen Thoughts
About Language*

ANDREA MORO

Translated from the Italian by Ian Roberts

COLUMBIA UNIVERSITY PRESS   NEW YORK

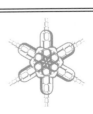

Columbia University Press
Publishers Since 1893
New York   Chichester, West Sussex
cup.columbia.edu
Copyright © 2016 Andrea C. Moro

Library of Congress Cataloging-in-Publication Data

Names: Moro, Andrea, author. | Roberts, Ian, translator.
Title: I speak, therefore I am : seventeen thoughts about language / Andrea Moro ;
    Translated from the Italian by Ian Roberts.
Other titles: Parlo dunque sono. English
Description: New York : Columbia University Press, [2016] | Translated from Italian:
    Parlo dungue sono, 2012. | Includes bibliographical references. | Description based
    on print version record and CIP data provided by publisher; resource not viewed.
Identifiers: LCCN 2015045115 (print) | LCCN 2015040186 (ebook) |
    ISBN 9780231533928 (electronic) | ISBN 9780231177405 (cloth : alk. paper) |
    ISBN 9780231177412 (pbk.)
Subjects: LCSH: Language and languages—Philosophy.
Classification: LCC P106 (print) | LCC P106 .M66513 2016 (ebook) | DDC401—dc23
LC record available at http://lccn.loc.gov/2015045115

Columbia University Press books are printed on permanent and durable acid-free paper.

Printed in the United States of America
c 10 9 8 7 6 5 4 3 2 1
p 10 9 8 7 6 5 4 3 2 1

Cover design: Phil Pascuzo

Break what break will! My mind abideth strong
To know the roots, how low soe'er they be,
Which grew to Oedipus. . . .
There is my lineage true, which none shall wrest
From me; who then am I to fear this quest?

—Sophocles, *Oedipus the King*, ll. 1076ff.

CONTENTS

PREFACE
Choice, Then Order, Then Chance, Finally Only Light

As any photographer knows, it takes hundreds, even thousands, of tries just to get one shot that's right. That's if everything goes well; sometimes, through dissatisfaction with a shot or an exposure that just can't capture that special moment, you just throw everything out. And then when the right photos have been chosen and put together in an album, you realize that the order in which they're placed makes a difference: a group of people sitting around a table followed by an empty mountain road means something different from an empty mountain road followed by a group of people sitting around a table. Maybe we can't quite say what it is, but we know there's a difference. Also, sometimes the best photo is the one taken by accident: all those carefully prepared, carefully worked-out efforts that were supposed to be masterpieces get thrown out, while just that one, taken by chance, may happen to capture that particular light or fix on that particular movement that alone make us relive a whole story.

Choice, then order, then chance: making a good photo album is really like doing science, because doing science, or doing it well, involves—and *has* to involve—all aspects of life. Science that tells us nothing about our-selves is useless, like a badly put-together photo album. And if we study language scientifically, it is impossible that we won't learn something about ourselves (unless we try not to), because language, like theorems and symphonies, exists only in us; outside of us, there are objects, motion, and light. Constellations and symphonies are there because we are there, look-ing and listening. And so it is for sentences; when we study sentences, we find ourselves, in a way, in the same situation as someone who studies light. We don't actually see light, we only see its effects on objects. We know it exists because it is partly reflected by the things it encounters, thereby making visible what would otherwise be invisible. In this way nothing, illuminated by another nothing, becomes, for us, something. Words and sentences work in the same way: they have no content of their own, but if they encounter someone who listens they become something. We are part of the data.

I SPEAK,

THEREFORE

I AM

1 GOD

And out of the ground the LORD God formed every beast of the field, and every fowl of the air; and brought them unto Adam to see what he would call them: and whatsoever Adam called every living creature, that was the name thereof.   —Genesis 2:19

In the beginning it might seem obvious to find Him, but in fact it isn't. Because, unexpectedly, God the Creator is a God who listens. The paradox is that language, our distinguishing characteristic above all other creatures, is in the first book of the Old Testament a gift that confirms beyond any doubt our freedom and our creativity. The consequences of this are made clear. We read that God created us in His image, but no one has ever seen the face of God. So what does it mean to say that we are created in His image? This is where language comes in. Perhaps our resemblance to God can be perceived in realizing we are able to give names to things. That is, the Creator has made us in His image because He recognizes our creations; although they are made only of air and thought, they are nonetheless creations: names. And not just any names: these are the names we give to *His* other creations. In the Jewish tradition, the God who created Man is the same God who stops and listens to Man naming things.

This is a kind of embryonic linguistics—names, not sentences—maybe "atomic" linguistics, but linguistics nonetheless. This is because thinking of and giving a name are not trivial acts. Names, in fact, are not just conventional labels: except in a few exceptional cases, nothing tells is that a given sound is right for a given name. This is obvious if we compare different languages, but, even leaving sounds aside, names are not just freely given conventional labels. For example, look at your hand. You instinctively recognize a natural object that can be broken down into parts: palm, fingers, knuckles, nails; we also give special names to the different fingers, funny names, childish names, noble or scientific names. In every language there are names for the pieces of what we see as making up a hand. But there are no tattoos marking the borders of these pieces: the combination of the fingertip and the distal phalange of a finger is an object in the real world too. Also, it is a coherent object, in the sense that it is not made of discontinuous pieces, just like the ring finger in relation to the whole hand. The difference is that in the second case there's a special name for the object, and in the first case there isn't.

Fortunately, we don't feel a need to give names to all the combinations of pieces of the world; sometimes it's convenient to invent names for *certain* things, but not for *every* possible combination of things. This is lucky, because the set of pieces of the world borders on uncountably infinite, and it would not be easy for a child to find themselves confronted with a percept of a wall made up of infinite subwalls, all of which have to be given a name. This would separate us forever from the city, because it would separate us from language, from what makes us human beings. What we need instead is a catalogue, capacious and partly elastic, but not infinite: in other words, a dictionary.

It would be good to catch our breath here, but we can't: talk of God and names leads inevitably to the endless tangle raised by the problem of His name. In the Jewish tradition, this is the *tetragrammaton*, a name that commands respect, whose pronounciation, never mind meaning, is unknown. We could perhaps leave the question aside, were it not for the fact that in the principal Christian prayer, the Lord's Prayer, which was based on a Jewish precursor, the name of God is immediately invoked. We say "Hallowed be Thy *name*"; that is, may the Lord's name be recognized as holy and treated as holy. So we have a God whom we can't (and wouldn't know how to) name, whose name features centrally in a prayer. It cannot be an accident that in that prayer there is a constant interplay between the pronouns "thou" and "we." Perhaps the name of God is to be found entirely in relation to us.

Continuing our ascent toward the name of God, we come across another, almost insurmountable obstacle. In the other tradition that forms the basis of our culture, the Greek tradition, the name (of the role) given to God is not "father," but *logos*. The *logos* is not only the beginning of everything but also what is made flesh. This word has been translated in different ways at different times, except when it has not been translated at all. Sometimes we use the simple word "word," sometimes the word by antonomasia, "verb," sometimes "number," sometimes "reason" (Zellini 2010). The only certain thing is that the root from which the word *logos* is formed originally alluded to the act of collecting, of putting chosen elements together in an organized way. Thus "anthology" is a "collection of flowers" and not "a discourse on flowers." Having said this, *logos* is meant to be made flesh: flesh, not something else. That is, our bodies, a blend of laws of nature and of history, are not only *compatible* with language but also an *inseparable expression* of it, and this is not at all accidental. We are thus made of the same substance as words, and so is God, who in this sense made us like Him: free, free to give names to things. We are all words made flesh.

So right from the start we see that thinking about language is a complicated, stormy, and mysterious business. For now, however, one certainty is clearly striking: however much veiled in mystery, the ability to name things is, as far as we are concerned, the real big bang that pertains to us.

2 PLATO

(Athens, 428–348 B.C.E.)

> So too some vocal signs do not harmonize, but some of them do harmonize and form discourse.
> —Plato, *The Sophist*

Here language becomes language, or rather linguistics becomes linguistics. We are no longer dealing with atoms in isolation—lists of names, as in the case of the Book of Genesis. Instead we are looking at combinations among atoms. This is the birth, or rather the recognition, of the most important molecules of words: sentences. At the same time it is recognized that not all combinations of words work. In this connection Plato uses the verb *harmóttein*, which we can translate as "to harmonize, to agree." But it is interesting to note that *harmóttein* comes from a different domain. For example, a carpenter assembling pieces of wood to make a stool would use this verb to say that one piece of wood fits better than another. Plato was aware of this, so much so that when he talks about words he begins with "so too," because just before he was giving exactly the example of how pieces of wood fit together. Fitting together means having two forms that are not only *compatible* but also *complementary*; that is, together they form something new that stands on its own. This means recognizing that language consists in harmony, of putting together parts in a way that is not random. This is the fundamental point regarding the structure of human language: it says that, starting from a set of primitive elements (whether sounds or words), not *all* combinations give rise to possible structures. It didn't take long to recognize this characteristic of language and give it a name: "syntax," i.e., composition (Graffi 2001, 2010). But it took more than two thousand years for linguists to recognize that these combinations manifest special mathematical properties that can be neither derived from experience nor constructed by chance, a result often ignored partly, due to a certain perverse tendency to privilege ideology over data (Berwick 1985; Chomsky 2012, 2013). The empirically based deductions concerning these mathematical properties are now established—later we will see some of them—and in some cases have the status of theorems. Continued attempts to dismantle and refute them are like trying to tickle a marble statue.

It should come as no surprise that the verb *harmóttein*, and the word "harmony" derived from it, are used in music, in art, in architecture, and in the theory where beauty matters, aesthetics. We can wonder why Plato used precisely this image and not a different one, but as Saussure once said in an unpublished note: "When we venture into the territory of language all the analogies in heaven and earth abandon us." Perhaps one image is as good as another; however, in talking about words, this attempt to convey the idea of the right combination in concrete, geometrical terms does not seem accidental. But if we look at language in particular, all kinds of different ways of fitting things together come to mind straightaway, all kinds of harmony: an article, for example, can harmonize with a noun, an auxiliary with a participle, a preposition with a verb, while still the mother of all linguistic harmonies is the agreement of noun and verb. In fact, Plato gives this case a special status, so special as to have it coincide with the essence of the *logos*, that is, discourse: that human reality, a uniquely human reality, made up of meanings, signifiers, and rules of combination. It is this reality that your eyes are seeing in a particular form, the written form, as they pass over this page at this very moment. You see it so naturally that it passes unnoticed, and yet it is so powerful and pervasive as to be able to evoke a mental image that has practically no probability of being predicted on the basis of the surrounding environment or the circumstances you are in at this moment, such as "a long line of lizards crossed the desert without even stopping to dream." Nobody can voluntarily fail to understand a sentence.

Plato doesn't explain to us what creates this harmony, but he presents it as intuitively obvious, and it is difficult to disagree with him in this. Even if we don't know how to define a noun, a verb, or a sentence, or if questions of linguistics do not interest us, we have no difficulty in recognizing the difference between two-word sequences such as "they thing" and "they think": in the second it seems that the words show a harmony missing in the first, whatever exactly we mean by "harmony." If, as Alfred North Whitehead said, all Western philosophy can be seen as a series of footnotes to the Platonic dialogues, the special harmony between nouns and verbs that creates discourse is one of the clearest examples of an original insight and, at the same time, of an idea that has persisted throughout Western thought in general: from linguistics to logic, from mathematics to artificial intelligence. The harmonic fit of nouns and verbs thus becomes the backbone of language and thought.

3 ARISTOTLE

(born Stageira 384 B.C.E.; died Euboea 322 B.C.E.)

For truth and falsity have to do with combination and separation.
—Aristotle, *De Interpretatione*

If I told you you were swallows, you would immediately object that that is not true. But then if I asked you what it means to say that it isn't true, the answer would not be so immediate. But everything is clear. Modern linguistics, armed with the weapons forged from logic and mathematics, tells us that a fundamental aspect of the meaning of a sentence like "All the readers of this book are swallows" is represented as a relation between two sets, the set of readers of this book and the set of swallows—a relation in which the set of readers of this book is contained in the set of swallows. To say that the sentence "All the readers of this book are swallows" is true or false then amounts, at a certain level of representation, to the possibility of saying whether this combination of the two sets associated with the sentence is correct. If the sentence had been "All the readers of this book are not swallows," on the other hand, this would have been a relation of separation: no individual in the first set is also in the second.

Aristotle tied the notion of truth—and therefore falsity—to language so closely that not even today, 2,300 years later, can we get away from treating the problem in these terms, although today the approach is constrained and enhanced by new techniques (see Chierchia 1995, Chierchia & McConnell 1995 for references). But, as everyone knows, Aristotle was Plato's pupil, and for Aristotle the bond between language and truth goes further, exploiting the knowledge of the harmonic fit between noun and verb recognized by his teacher. In fact, Aristotle said that there are no combinations or separations—and hence truth or falsity—without the combination of noun and verb, or, more precisely, subject and predicate. It seems that we are saying the same thing using different words: "subject" instead of "noun," and "predicate" instead of "verb"—but it's not so. The analogy between noun and verb on the one hand and subject and predicate on the other breaks down when we bring into consideration, in Greek and other languages that have it, the verb "to be." Why? Let us proceed step by step. When he tried to find a way to define a sentence, Aristotle realized that it isn't possible to give a general account: sentences can be used, for example, to order, to ask, to beg, to pray, to be ironic, to hypothesize, to implore, and to describe. So, for various reasons connected above all with his interest in deductive reasoning, Aristotle concentrated on this last fundamental capacity of language and stated that a sequence of words is a sentence only if it means something true or false. So, "that woman thinks" is a sentence, but "that woman who thinks" isn't. In this way, he goes on to put logical flesh on the Platonic bones of noun-verb agreement. He distinguishes between that *which* is attributed and that to *which* something is attributed. That something to which a property is attributed is the thing that exists underneath all the properties given to it: it is "the thing that stands underneath," "the sub-stance" or, in linguistic terms, the "subject." These are all terms whose etymology reveals a "stereoscopic" view of reality. And for the property attributed to the substance Aristotle uses the term designating the accused in a trial or in speeches in the public square, the *agorà*: *categoroúmenon* or, in Boethius's Latin translation, "predicate," to speak in front of others. Subject and predicate, then, are the two pillars of linguistic, logical, ontological, and mathematical thought: without these, there would be no rational thought. And, as in the case of harmonic agreement between noun and verb, no one has managed to derive these properties from simpler facts (yet).

But now let's go back to the verb "to be," if only very briefly. Aristotle saw that in order to have a sentence a subject and a predicate weren't enough; a verb is needed too. But why? Aren't verbs predicates? No: Aristotle realized that in his language (and in our too) *not all* verbs are predicates, or rather that there is one verb that is not a predicate of anything, a verb that does not express any kind of property—the verb "to be." This is a verb whose only function is to express tense, which is obligatorily applied as a third element alongside a subject and a predicate to make a sentence when tense cannot be expressed by means of the predicate. For example: just as I can say "A picture on the wall was the cause of the riot," so I can say "A picture on the wall caused the riot." In one case the verbal inflection (-d) expresses tense along with the property (cause-); in the other, since the predicate is a noun (cause), in order to express tense we need a verb "empty" of meaning, but nonetheless able to indicate tense (was). But the story of the verb "to be" is long, tortuous, and complicated, involving the logical duels of the Middle Ages, the battle over the mechanical nature of thought a few centuries later in the Baroque era, and leading up to the mathematics of the nineteenth and twentieth centuries. This story would take up at least a whole separate album (see Moro 2010 for a history of "be" and the appendix of Moro 1997 for a sketchy version).

For now, let's just take note of the bond between language and truth proposed in Aristotle and the related possibility of investigating language as the tool of logic. Even today, this bond is not quite fully frozen in place.

4 MARCUS TERENTIUS VARRO

(born Rieti 116 B.C.E.; died Rome 27 C.E.)

I call it nature, when we all accept a name but do not ask of the one who
set it how he wishes it to be inflected, but ourselves inflect it.

—Varro, *Varro on the Latin Language*

Everyone knows that "the onx cannipted the snacknercasters." But if we
want to talk about more than one onx, we don't have to ask anyone how
to say it. We know perfectly well that it is "the onxes cannipted the snacknercasters." We are not in the least surprised, even if we have never heard
of "onxes," "snacknercasters," or "cannipting," and even if we have no idea
what these words might mean. And if children, having heard by chance
that someone has baked something, tell us that someone else has "taked"
something, we should give them a prize, because they have constructed a
perfect analogical proportion on their own: "baked" stands to "bake" as
"taked" stands to "take." But in fact we immediately feel obliged to tell her
that we don't live in the best of all possible worlds and, despite all reasonable expectations, some words show anomalous behavior. Varro is telling

us explicitly that part of our knowledge is not taught to us, it comes from nature. This observation might seem trivial to many people, but in fact it points to a central question that is not obvious at all, neither in Varro's time nor today. I do not think it an exaggeration to say that this tension between analogy and anomaly in language, which for certain philologists of the Hellenistic period became radicalized in the dispute between the Alexandrine School in Egypt and the Pergamon School in Asia Minor (Lesky 1971), constitutes the fundamental dispute among different theoretical models of reality.

On the one hand, the meaning of things—their "structure," as we would perhaps say nowadays—is seen as emerging from an unformed, infinite magma through the spontaneous development of symmetrical relations (analogy); on the other hand, structure would be formed by unforseen and unforeseeable fractures in an immense lattice of symmetrical regularities, where everything would be otherwise inert, as it would be everywhere the same (anomaly). I have never been able to find anything more general than the contrast between anomalists and analogists: the entire world seems to me to be describable in one way or the other, *tertium non datur.* The point is that I can't decide whether to say "and" or "or": "in one way *and* the other" or "in one way *or* the other." Actually, the difficulty is just the result of a much deeper indecision: I can't tell whether analogy and anomaly are ways the world is organized or ways our way of seeing the world is organized. To tell the truth, I gave up on this problem some time ago: aside from not being able to solve it, I wouldn't even know whom to ask for an expert opinion. However, I do know that asking whether *the world* is organized according to analogy or anomaly is different from asking whether *language* is organized one way or the other. This distinction isn't hard to understand, because behind it is the idea that the structure of human language, that is to say the elements that make up language and the rules that combine these elements to form more complex structures, does not derive (or at least not completely) from the structure of the world. In brief, we could have an "anomalous" world and "analogous" language, or an "anomalous" language and an "analogous" world. All of this wouldn't be very relevant, or even very interesting, were it not for the fact that language wouldn't exist at all but for the activity of one thing (or really one thing for each person) in the world: the human brain.

Unfortunately, in this context the greatest scientific revolution regarding spontaneous child-language acquisition not only doesn't help, it actually radicalizes the division between these two opposing visions of reality. I'm talking about the second half of the twentieth century, when for the first time a theory of language acquisition was developed, on the basis of Noam Chomsky's work, which opposed traditional ideas (Chomsky 2004; Graffi 2001, 2010). The hypothesis that the formal rules of the mother tongue (understood to include all the subcomponents of grammar, including syntax) are built up out of nothing was replaced by the hypothesis that human beings are born with a brain that (potentially) contains all possible grammars. Learning is then not a process of *construction*, but of *selection* (Piatelli-Palmarini 1989); the grammars that the child is not exposed to atrophy and die, so to speak; the grammar that survives the weeding-out process stabilizes and becomes the grammar of our native language (or languages, in the case of multilingualism). This process, for which Jacques Mehler coined the term "learning by forgetting" (Mehler 1974), seems also promising for research in neuropsychology, because it can be interpreted as the reflex of the progressive reduction in the synaptic contacts in the child's brain, famously studied by Changeux (Changeux et al. 1975). However, so far no one has managed to measure these reductions, or to explain them as a consequence of language acquisition, or for that matter of other cognitive capacities. It is obvious that the distance between linguistic regularities and neurobiological observations is in this case (still) overwhelming, and that we don't know how to give new content of a neurobiological kind to the opposition between anomaly and analogy (see Moro 2015). In fact, whether learning corresponds to the formation and stabilization of synaptic connections in a labyrinth of chaotic circuits or it rather involves closing certain circuits in a symmetric lattice, the fundamental problem remains unsolved, although the possible outlines of a solution are starting to emerge from the fog of myth.

Perhaps the tension between analogy and anomaly isn't a problem. Perhaps it is the engine driving our thoughts. In any case, one fact remains that everyone intuitively recognizes: there's something in language that, as Varro said, we know "on our own."

5 ROGER BACON

(born Ilchester ca. 1213; died Oxford 1294)

Grammatica una et eadem est secundum substantiam in omnibus linguis, licet accidentaliter varietur.

[Jacobson: "Grammar is, in its essence, one and the same in all languages, even though it differs in superficial features."]

—Bacon, *Grammatica Greca*

Apparently, but only apparently, Bacon seems to have reached one of the major conclusions of linguistic theory of the second half of the twentieth century seven hundred years earlier: that is, that there is just one human language determined by its substance; the differences among languages are superficial accidents. Babel is then reduced to an optical illusion, just as in a certain sense the heterogeneous multitude of different species is an optical illusion, since today we know that these are all variations of a single genetic code. However, it's not so: Bacon followed a totally different course to arrive in apparently the same place, a rich and strange land that, surprisingly, is reemerging today and may require us to navigate a new course.

Meanwhile we have to understand how Bacon arrived at his conclusion: obviously not on the basis of empirical evidence. In the Middle Ages the modern notion of empirical evidence had not yet been developed. In that otherwise enlightened time, however, the dominant philosophical tradition provided a different motivation for his conclusion. The central dogma on which Bacon based his thinking consists in the assumption that the *modes* in which we interpret reality, the *modes* in which signs represent reality, and the *modes* in which objects and facts exist reflect one another in cosmic unity. This tradition, known as the "Modistic" tradition, gave rise to a particular kind of linguistics, known as "speculative" grammar, which was explicitly contrasted with "practical" grammar, suggesting to some an imaginative but suggestive etymology according to which the term "speculative" has to do with the ability of grammar to reflect the world, exactly as in a mirror (Pinborg 1982, Graffi 2010).[1] And since the modes of existence are obviously universal, despite linguistic variation, it follows that the modes in which grammar is organized are also universal: differences can only therefore be accidental. It doesn't matter that this conclusion is reached without empirical evidence; what does matter here is to bring out the core thesis: that language *reflects* the world. This is a very tricky point. Surprisingly, it is exactly this idea that we can now decide on the basis of empirical arguments, thus determining our conception of language, and therefore of the human mind and the human species. Let us go step by step.

If there's just one star in the sky and I call it "star," I'm applying an arbitrary label to a thing in the world. If I see two stars, I call them "stars." In our language, an -s at the end of the word tells me if there is more than one of something, analogously to other words like "frog/frogs"; it is hard to deny that the plural is a way of incorporating something (from our perceptions) of the world into our grammar. Obviously it's an accident that a final −s indicates plural: in Italian, for example, there is a change in the final vowel of the noun (*stella* "star"; *stelle* "stars"); other words use different vowels (*anatroccolo* "duckling"; *anatroccoli* "ducklings"). The real problem is a different and much deeper one, and it picks up on Bacon's core thesis: is it possible that all the regularities of human languages not due to chance are incorporating into grammar (from our perceptions) some property of the world? There are many reasons for giving a negative answer to this question, especially in the domain of syntax (Tettamanti & Moro 2012; see also Hickok 2014), and therefore to radically refute Bacon's motivation for his conclusion, which looked so similar to the ideas of late twentieth-century linguistics.

Bacon couldn't have known, but at the heart of the syntax of all human languages are mathematical properties that it would be difficult to derive from the structure of the world. For example, and this is something we will return to, among these properties are procedures that are (potentially) infinitely iterable (Chomsky 1956, Hopcroft et al. 2006). This represents a great challenge, and it is not clear how to face up to it. We could start by looking for a counterexample and ask ourselves what properties would convince us that syntax cannot be derived from the structure of the world. Certainly, if we found a syntactic rule that was based on prime numbers, then that diabolical grammar could by definition not be derived from the structure of the world, because (at least if certain quantum physicists are right—see Derbyshire 2003) nothing in nature patterns the way prime numbers pattern. In any case, even if we don't have this kind of diabolical proof, there are other proofs we can take advantage of.

Alongside the class of properties that refer to infinity, which as already mentioned we'll come back to soon, there's at least one other that we can use precisely because it relates directly to Bacon's core thesis that language reflects the facts of the world. This property is one of the most surprising features of language: the ability to produce negative sentences, such as "Big Ben is not in New York." In fact, negation is an exclusively linguistic property, because there is no sense in talking about "negative stimuli" or "false facts": that is, there is no unambiguous stimulus that corresponds to the fact that Big Ben is *not* in New York, although there can be unfulfilled expectations (Big Ben used to be in New York but it's been moved, or it would be nice if Big Ben were in New York) and an infinite number of facts that are compatible with this sentence, but the only true fact is that Big Ben is in London.

What has negation got to do with the refutation of the idea that language "incorporates" the world? The link between these two points is somewhat indirect and is not intuitive, or perhaps even cogent. But it seems to me to bring about a new idea. The motivation comes from an experiment: using neuroimaging techniques, we were able to show that negation—a purely linguistic fact—activates cerebral circuits involved in the representation of sentences about motor actions. Of course, linguistics, like any empirical science, doesn't *demonstrate* anything; we can only try to collect data that *favor* a given hypothesis, but the negation data make the hypothesis that *all* of the structure of human language can be explained as the incorporation of the structure of the world into grammar highly implausible (Tettamanti et al. 2008a, Tettamanti & Moro 2012). In particular, they support the idea of the primacy of grammar over perception and the organization of movement, contrary to certain other proposals (Corballis 2003). The burden of proof now falls on those who wish to uphold the (motor planning and perceptual) reductionist position.

Notice that saying that grammar is not shaped by the world by no means rules out the possibility that language is physically supported. In fact, it is. Language as a physical object lives in two different domains: outside our skull and inside it. Curiously, in both domains it has the shape of waves: mechanical waves of air, i.e., sound waves, which carry the information from one mouth to one or more ears through the air; electrical waves among networks of cells, which is the way neurons compute information in complex networks.[2] Neurophysiological studies have shown that when we hear sentences the electrophysiological activity of the brain preserves the sound in formation in a tonotopic way, i.e., the distinct components of the sound are separated and computed in distinct areas in the brain, after having being processed by the ear. This may not be too surprising, although it could well have been the case that sound waves could be too hard to recognize once the sound is translated into electrical waves. But what happens when our language is confined within our skull, that is, when we read silently—as you are probably doing now—or just elaborate thoughts in our mind? My colleagues and I have tried to answer this question by means of an experiment (see Magrassi et al. 2015 and Moro 2015 for a nontechincal illustration of this and related experiments): by exploiting the so-called "awake surgery technique"—where the patient's cortex is temporary exposed for therapeutic reasons (see Calvin–Ojemann [1994])—we have measured the electric activity of the neurons in *nonacoustic* areas (in particular, Broca's area) and compared the case-when patients heard someone saying or reading aloud a given sentence to the case when they were reading it in their mind silently, that is, without any sound emission. The result was surprising: the neurons' electric activity was practically identical in both cases, showing that (in normal hearing people) sound representation is not just the superficial and peripheral disguise of an otherwise completely mysterious activity but rather inherently entangled with the generation and computation of linguistic structures (also showing different responses between stimuli made of isolated words versus full-fledged sentences). A first crack has been made in the secret electric code neurons use to compute our linguistic thought. With neuroimaging we understood *where* computations take place; with electrophysiology we are starting to decipher *what* computations are made of, approaching neurolinguistics in the true sense for the first time, as hoped for in Poepple (1996).

Notably, not only does this result give empirical justification to the subjective sensation of inner speech, it also paves the way to accessing our linguistic thought by directly measuring the electrical activity of the brain, with obvious interesting and worrisome consequences for clinical, evolutionary, and ethical issues along with purely linguistic ones. Our sentences are made of the same stuff waves are made of, and they appear to have the same shape inside and outside us.

Returning to a point raised earlier in relation to Bacon, as far as the belief that we can *only* get to firm conclusions the empirical way is concerned, some people may be surprised—as I was—to learn that Galileo never wasted his time dropping objects of different weights from the Tower of Pisa and making complicated measurements. Reason alone sufficed for him to understand that objects take the same amount of time to reach the ground: if a light object and a heavy object took different amounts of time, then if you tied them together you'd be forced to the paradoxical conclusion that the lighter one would slow the heavier one down independently of the increase in overall weight. Clearly, the contribution of reason and evidence to understanding the world has a variable geometry.

6 DESCARTES

(born La Haye-en-Touraine 1596;
died Stockholm 1650)

There are no men so dull and stupid, not even idiots, as to be incapable of joining together different words, and thereby constructing a declaration by which to make their thoughts understood; and . . . on the other hand, there is no other animal, however perfect or happily circumstanced which can do the like. —Descartes, *Discourse on the Method*, Part V

The content of this quotation can't be trivial, since four centuries later it was firmly reasserted at the Plenary Lecture of the Linguistics Society of America by the society's president, Stephen Anderson: "All other animal communication systems are based on a limited and fixed set of discrete messages, almost exclusively limited to the here and now. The inventory of these messages in each species constitutes a fixed list which cannot be expanded by combining elements to form more complex messages." There are two distinct sources of possible confusion here. The first consists in confusing the *ability* to communicate with the *structure* of the code used in communication. Certainly, all animals communicate: hummingbirds with hummingbirds, ants with ants, dogs with dogs, cats with cats, dogs with cats, hummingbirds with cats, and so on. Of course, if communicating just means transferring information from one individual to another, then even a poppy can communicate with another poppy by exchanging pollen, but it's difficult to admit that there is, in any nonmetaphorical sense, a language of poppies. The case of animals is trickier, above all because it's obvious that there are animals that think and communicate (even symbolically, as when cats use their urine to mark their territory; but see Tattersal 2012); so for those who link thought and communication to language without making further distinctions, it's difficult to avoid the conclusion that these animals have language.

On the other hand, if we concentrate on the *structure* of language, that is, the structure of the code that bears information, then the difficulties disappear, at least for anyone who approaches the question empirically. The most striking case was the famous experiment carried out on a baby chimp (Terrace et al. 1979). In the 1970s a group of researchers lived apart from other humans but with a baby chimp and communicated (among themselves and with the chimp) exclusively in American Sign Language. They compared the development of the baby chimp with that of a human baby. This was a decisive move, aimed at overcoming once and for all the insistent (and baseless) objection that chimps can't speak because of the configuration of their larynx and other organs of speech compared to those of humans. The result was clear: at the beginning, the linguistic development of the chimp and the child were substantially parallel. Both attained mastery of a vocabulary of about 120 words; then, suddenly, the child started using word order to express different, subtle, and ever more complex meanings. To us this is a completely natural phenomenon, so much so that we don't even notice it. With three words, such as "Cain," "Abel" and "killed," we can formulate two sentences with opposing meanings: "Cain killed Abel" and "Abel killed Cain." This property of our code, which we call "syntax," is something chimpanzees just don't have. But it's not just a question of the order of presentation of nouns and verbs. Let me give an example: English children can formulate simple two-word sentences with no verb, like "Daddy here" (meaning "Daddy is here") or "hat red" (meaning "the hat is red"); but when they start to produce three-word sentences, like "Daddy hat here" (meaning "Daddy's hat is here"), they are making a quantum leap. No new words are used; just the syntax gives rise to the new meaning (here the meaning of possession). This is one of many similar cases that show that the human baby outstrips the baby chimp.

These days it is taken to be established that syntax constitutes the principal difference between the human communicative code and those of all other animals (Anderson 2008). Starting from this result, research continues on three distinct but connected aspects of syntactic structure, which constitute major challenges, and not just for linguistics.

The first challenge is to explicitly and rigorously work out the elementary mathematical properties that make complex structures possible, in particular those potentially infinitely iterable basic procedures that generate hierarchical structures, which are then linearized as sequences of words, for example sentences that in their turn contain other sentences, which contain sentences, etc. (this is the theory of recursion).[1]

The second challenge is to capture in formal terms the limits to syntactic variation *across* languages (the theory of parameters) and *within* languages (the theory of locality), thereby reducing variation to invariant principles (Rizzi 1990, 2009; Manzini 1992; Longobardi & Roberts 2010). It's important to point out that the theory of locality, which acts as a filter on the recursive structure generated by the elementary procedures, is based solely on hierarchical rather than linear relations; this interplay between construction and selection on a recursive basis is the defining characteristic of all, and only, human grammars. Even if we were to find a recursive animal communication system or a self-organizing artificial system (neural networks, for example) lacking in selective filters, this kind of communication system would still not even be close to human languages in terms of complexity, as it would lack locality principles.

The third challenge is to understand how this recursive-selective code can *only* be realized in a human brain, on the basis of functional neurobiological mechanisms that we are just beginning to get a glimpse of (Moro 2013, 2015).

In any case, it *must* be the structure of language that makes us different from other animals. We are the only species in which each individual does not have to remake the whole of history, from the beginning, all alone. In other words, we can experience progress: we don't invent the wheel at age two, fire at age six, electricity at twenty-one; every one of us starts from what others have already discovered. This isn't true for spiders: a spider spins its web exactly as its father and grandfather did; the webs are perfect (Levi-Montalcini 1987), very complicated, but practically identical. Of course, writing, which surprisingly is also based on dedicated neurobiological networks (Dehaene 2009, Magrassi et al. 2010), is important, but it's not indispensable. Given these premises, the conclusion that history and progress are consequences of the structure of language—and not of communication *per se*—is almost unavoidable.

I hope this is an adequate answer to the question whether animals can speak. If not, I can only refer to Alan Turing, who, in a different context, said, "The original question (can machines think?), I take to be so devoid of meaning as to not merit discussion. Nonetheless, I think that by the end of this century language usage and educated opinion that we will be able to talk about intelligent machines without expecting to be contradicted" (Turing 1950). I think the same holds here too: the danger lies in extending the use of the word "speak" to the point where it would apply not just to chimps but also to poppies.

7

ANTOINE ARNAULD

(born Paris 1612; died Brussels 1694)

CLAUDE LANCELOT

(born Paris 1615; died Quimperlé 1695)

> Men are naturally inclined to abbreviate their expressions.
> —Arnauld and Lancelot, *Grammaire*

One might reasonably suspect that laziness is a widespread personality trait. But it is not at all obvious that a noble variant of this same trait has a decisive influence on the structure of language. It has to be shown. When Arnauld and Lancelot put forward the principle quoted above in their *Grammaire*, one of the cardinal texts in the history of Western linguistics, they had in mind cases reminiscent of Aristotle, such as the contrast between "Peter caused the riot" and "Peter was the cause of the riot": normally, however, tense is expressed in the same word as the predicate in the form of verbal inflection (caused), so we have one word instead of three (was the cause). For example, we don't say, "Peter is the walker," but rather "Peter walks." This principle looks quite straightforward, but actually has very general and pervasive effects and leads to extraordinary and surprising theoretical consequences. Let us see why.

Another example of the "abbreviation" (or economy) principle is illustrated by Arnauld and Lancelot with the sentence "Invisible God created the visible world," which they analyze as the combination of three simpler sentences: "God is invisible," "God created the world," "the world is visible." Here we can readily see one of the most important general precepts of Cartesian philosophy at work: the complex is the result of the interaction of simpler elements. Language too can be analyzed following this compositional principle. And there are many examples of this, such as the inclusion of a sentence inside another sentence. Instead of conjoining two sentences and saying "Joshua lives in Manhattan" and "Joshua is going to see the Seagram Building," we prefer to say "Joshua, who lives in Manhattan, is going to see the Seagram Building." This type of "abbreviation"— one sentence (a relative clause) inside another (a main clause)—illustrates to the naked eye a characteristic strategy of all and only human languages: a structure of a certain type, contained in a structure of the *same* type, sometimes referred to as "nested structures."

The kind of "Russian doll" effect is known more technically as "recursion," and it has at least two extremely significant consequences. The first, and obvious, one is that the relation between two words in a sentence never depends on a fixed distance (because it is always possible to introduce other words organized in their turn in a syntactically acceptable way). The second, which is not obvious at all, is that in syntactic structures the only thing that really counts is the relation between structures embedded inside one another, not the order in which the words are placed. In this case too a simple example illustrates how things are. If I say "John runs," I've clearly made the correct agreement between the two words; if I say instead "John run," I've produced a sequence without agreement, a disharmonic string. But is it always true that the string "John run" is unacceptable? No: natural languages have a surprising property. An unacceptable string can be made acceptable if it is preceded (or followed) by the "right" other words. In our example, the right words are "people who know." Adding these words makes "John run" acceptable, in fact perfect: "People who know John run." What matters here is the long-distance relation between "people" and "run." The embedded sentence (who know John) doesn't count at all for the agreement with the verb "run"; it's as if it weren't there. And obviously this process can go on indefinitely: "People who my sister claims love John run, People who Fred says my sister claims love John run," and so on, putting an ever greater distance and more nested structures between "people" and "run" (subject only to memory limitations). One of the most fascinating and promising research questions in contemporary linguistics involves reducing all syntactic rules to recursive relations, which also characterize two other specifically human cognitive domains: mathematics and music. Of course we don't know whether or how these recursive formal relations might be isomorphic to effectively recursive processes at the neuropsychological level, although some tentative experimental results are starting to provide some positive support for this hypothesis (Abutalebi et al. 2007; Pallier et al. 2011; Moro 2011a).

Coming back to the abbreviation principle with which we began, this also gives us a way to see that another force, in a sense of an opposite kind, is operative in language. Let's take as our example a sequence of words like "This boy runs, dances, hops, and skips." Here the same information, that the subject is singular, is repeated five times: by the form of the demonstrative "this" (as opposed to "these") and by the –s ending on all four verbs. The opposing force can be seen with the naked eye, and it is just as pervasive: this is the principle of superabundance of information, so-called "redundancy" (see de Mauro 2007 and the references given there).

But redundancy isn't at all in conflict with recursion. Therefore, grammar doesn't rely just on laziness but also on generous repetition. But that's not all: the economy principle runs into difficulties in relation to other facts, such as the (mistaken, but intuitively plausible) idea that pronouns are just another way of saving our breath. Thus, it has been said that instead of saying "The woman that Dante loves thinks that the woman that Dante loves is beautiful," we say "The woman that Dante loves thinks that she is beautiful." But in fact there are counterexamples, known as "Bach-Peters sentences," that falsify the general hypothesis that pronouns are interpreted as substitutes. Let us take for example the sentence "The woman who married him thinks that the man who loves her is crazy": if the interpretation of the pronouns were obtained by substituting the pronouns with the series of words to which they refer, we would come to an infinite regress and would never be able to understand the sentence, contrary to fact.

We have to resign ourselves to the fact that language, like many other aspects of nature, is neither all synthesis nor all redundancy, but shows an equilibrium between the two. What is certain is that the abbreviation principle takes us straight to a leading idea of enormous heuristic value: that complexity results from the interaction of simple parts even in the domain of the mental.

8 SIR WILLIAM JONES

(born London 1746; died Calcutta 1794)

No philologer could examine them [Sanskrit, Greek, and Latin] all three, without believing them to have sprung from some common source, which, perhaps, no longer exists.

—Jones, presidential address to the Royal Asiatick Society
of Bengal, February 2, 1786

If you're at a wedding and you notice two people who look very similar, it's natural to think that they're related. Nothing odd about that. It's different if, on a trip to the other side of the world, you run into someone who looks just like your next-door neighbor. Here's a dilemma: either the resemblance is purely accidental or they are related. Like comes from like, as everyone knows, but here we're saying something more: the two people who look alike *must* come from the same ancestor. If you were sufficiently curious or if this were a detective story, you'd try to solve the mystery of the *Doppelgänger*; you'd start to investigate and to map out their family trees. That is, you'd start searching for something unknown, because the data that you've got are enough to convince you that there has to be something behind the mystery.

But science, one might object, isn't a detective story: science measures what exists in the here and now. Is that true? No. This is the great value of Jones's intuition: there are objective data that become comprehensible only if the way is opened up to the analysis of what no longer exists, the reconstruction of what must have been there earlier on the basis of what remains now. Perhaps it doesn't seem like saying very much, but all of science lies hidden behind this quotation, except for mathematics (quite reasonably). Besides, today's fragments would not even be comprehensible if they weren't connected to the story of the past.

For linguistics it was a sudden, unheard-of leap: it wasn't enough to know, as had been known for centuries, that alongside the classical languages one had to study the vernaculars, as well as all the languages that had left any trace; now linguists realized that it was important to study languages of which nothing remained, except what was imprinted in other languages, as in the case of Indo-European. In this way, languages were proposed whose very existence represented a way to understand the data. In this way, whole new worlds, reconstructed on the basis of a few clues, were suddenly and unexpectedly opened up. It's certainly a natural human tendency to start from a few details and construct whole words on that basis; Tolkien did this, in building a whole epic around the languages he'd invented, in a way perhaps not so dissimilar from the archaeologist who discovers an arm, a skull, and a shoulder blade and reconstructs a whole Hercules. In linguistics this tendency was elevated to a method. Anyone can see how in this case linguistics was a precursor to post-Linnean biology, not so much in giving a central heuristic role to comparison, but in legitimating the reconstruction of the elements at the origin of the diversity of the present. Of course, history has always been based on following up on clues, but this is something else: it's as if in reconstructing the history of Europe and the history of Asia we came to postulate the existence of a lost continent, the only proof of whose existence would lie in the resemblance between things in the present that cannot be seen as purely accidental.

What is left today of this experiment? In addition to the enormous amount of comparative data (collected mainly for Indo-European and mainly by German linguists in the nineteenth century), we are left with the knowledge that the comparison and reconstruction of what no longer exists on the basis of present resemblances is a fully legitimate scientific methodology. Today, in the era of neuroimaging, comparison remains an essential heuristic technique, but—as we will see later—we are no longer restricted to comparing real (and distant) languages; we can try to compare "possible" and "impossible" languages (see Moro 2015 for a nontechnical illustration and Moro 2013 for a collection of papers pertaining to this issue), in the reasonable and often-fulfilled hope that by comparing the possible with the impossible we'll get a glimpse of that tiny space from which we can begin to unravel the structure of reality.

9
HERMANN OSTHOFF
(born Unna 1847; died Heidelberg 1909)
E. KARL BRUGMANN
(born Wiesbaden 1849; died Leipzig 1919)

Every sound change, since it proceeds mechanically, follows exception-less laws. —Osthoff and Brugmann, *Morphologische Untersuchungen*

Perhaps it's just a personal quirk, but I am absolutely fascinated by the internal workings of a watch. The gears seem endowed with a life of their own, but in fact we know that every cog and every lever moves as the effect of a series of purely mechanical causes and, even more importantly, that everything is always inexorably going in the same predetermined direction: there are no choices. We have to be careful not to get too entranced by this vision; there's a danger that we'll see life where there is no life. The opposite can also happen: there are cases where instead of diffuse and unpredictable vitality we see rigid schemata that close our eyes to the reality.

Osthoff and Brugmann's intuition hauls linguistics up into the exclusive heights of logic and formal reasoning for the first time, by making the notion of law relevant to linguistics, as it is for the other empirical sciences (Feynman 1967). In his essay on the character of physical law Richard Feynman shows how tricky this notion really is in the hard sciences, but in the nineteenth century the proposal that language obeys mechanical laws was as surprising as it would be today if someone showed that a painting is a statistical notion. True, they were "only" talking about sound laws—when a given sound is in a given phonetic context in a word with a given stress pattern, then that sound will in time be subject to the same changes as other comparable ones—but these were really and truly laws. This was an epoch-making intuition (Graffi 2010), and linguistics is still dealing with its consequences. Language as a machine, deterministically structured according to laws that do not admit exceptions. This perspective was extended to other domains; for a while in the first half of the twentieth century, it was believed that even child language acquisition was the result of a gigantic, extremely complex stimulus, so complex, in fact, as to be inexplicable even in its own terms and hence useless, like a map that contains every detail of the territory it describes (Chomsky 1959). This journey along the tracks of automatism as a model of the mind was inevitably derailed when the illusory idea of a machine that by simulating it, could explain the structure of language began to be understood. Yehoshua Bar-Hillel, talking about the MIT Electronic Laboratory in the 1950s, admitted despite himself that "in the lab there was a general and irresistible conviction that with the new field of cybernetics and the recent techniques in information theory we had arrived at the last stage before a complete understanding of animal and machine communication." The mirage dissolved when the young Noam Chomsky showed that, as in the physical sciences, the laws of language, and particularly of syntax, must be explored with patience and tenacity in the knowledge that whatever is discovered is only valid "until proved wrong"; that a theory must be globally evaluated in terms of the predictions it makes and its overall simplicity relative to other theories; and, finally, that simulating doesn't mean understanding, just as getting a computer to perform a calculation doesn't necessarily tell us how the brain calculates (without of course in any way detracting from the enormous advantages of being able to build machines that can simulate aspects of human behavior).[1]

The introduction of the notion of law into linguistics has nonetheless left a huge legacy, although this isn't always properly evaluated. One of the clearest positive effects that can be enumerated is the definitive emancipation of linguistics from the dubious realm of the erudite anecdote (aside from a few tenacious enclaves) and its growing orientation toward the empirical sciences. However, among its dubious effects is one that is in fact not logically connected to the introduction of the notion of law into linguistics, although for unclear reasons it is often connected to that: the idea that the existence of a law should be accounted for in terms of the function it carries out. In reality, laws have coherence and force, but there is no necessary reason for them to be functional. On the contrary, nowadays it seems much more reasonable to say that internally to a system, a function depends entirely on the elements that interface with that system. From this point of view, even the relation between the formal properties of language and their neurobiological substrate can be seen as accidental. Chomsky: "If [the lexical items and linguistic expressions] were embedded in different performance systems in some hypothetical (perhaps biologically impossible) organism, they could serve as instructions for other activity, say, locomotion." This may seem to be a very radical view, but actually there's nothing really new about it, at least outside linguistics. As early as the nineteenth century, Emil Du Bois-Reymond, discussing the sensory systems, wrote: "With the nerves of vision and of hearing severed, and then crossed with each other, we should with the eye hear the lightning-flash as a thunder-clap, and with the ear we should see the thunder as a series of luminous impressions" (Du Bois-Reymond 1874). So there's no functional *raison d'être* even for the sensory organs, then. The same must be true for other areas, *mutatis mutandis*.

Language remains a genuine mystery: it is made from flesh and yet obeys mathematical laws. All we can do at present is describe its structure and its limits, which is rather like describing the palette that produces a painting. The painting itself remains a total mystery but that doesn't mean that we have to consider the palette to be mystery too.

10 FERDINAND DE SAUSSURE

(born Geneva 1857; died Vufflens-le-Château, 1913)

In language there are only differences.
—Saussure, *Cours de linguistique générale*

Imagine any kind of catalogue. Each element in the catalogue is distinguished according to whatever properties are recognized as relevant. This is certainly a natural way of organizing a description: one puts together a list of properties that characterize every element in the set. So, for example, if you have ten bicycles, you can describe each one in terms of its color, the type of wheel, the saddle cover, the shape of the handlebars, and so on. It's likely that the ten bicycles will be quite different from one another in relation to the properties chosen; that they won't all have the same color, the same type of wheel, the same saddle cover, the same handlebar shape, etc. However, imagine that after taking a longer look at the same ten bikes you notice that in certain ways there are relations among their properties. For example, five of the bikes have racing handlebars and the other five don't: having handlebars is obviously a property of all the bikes, but having racing handlebars is a property of only five of them. Imagine now that we notice another property: five of the bikes have flat tires and five do not, and maybe this division doesn't correspond to the one based on the type of handlebars. Carrying on in this way, we reach a descriptive situation completely different from the one we started with: if we're really lucky, with just four properties defined for each bike we can characterize every one of them uniquely. So if we label the properties A, B, C, D, with, for example, +A meaning the bike has a certain property (e.g., racing handlebars), and −A meaning that the bike in question doesn't have that property, we can construct 16 (2⁴) different combinations: the bike type [+A, +B, +C, +D], the bike type [-A, +B, +C, +D], and so on until we've exhausted all the combinations.

Three points are worth making about this system. First, we'd have to be really lucky, because it's not obvious that we'd be able to find four properties that divide the bikes into two different groups every time (we might need more properties). Second, given that there are ten bikes and the combinations of our four properties give sixteen classes, that means that there are six types of bike that are not in our group—maybe it would be worth looking for them. Third, in the differential grids that we construct in this way, not *all* the properties of a member count (assuming that the list of properties can in any case ever be exhaustive); the only thing that counts is how the member of the group is characterized in relation to the properties chosen.

Coming back to our example, any bike of type [+A, +B, +C, +D] is fine; in other words, when a member is characterized in the given way in relation to the chosen properties, any other element having the same characterization in relation to those properties can be substituted (technically, *commuted*) for that member of the group. Moreover, using grids of this kind, it often turns out that there are subsets of members that can be identified by a smaller number of properties than the number of elements in the subset so defined; these are called "natural classes." Often these natural classes are what is really interesting, and they can give us a simpler explanation of the facts. This type of classification was developed and used to classify the sounds of language; for example, we speak [+voice] or [-voice] consonants in pairs like *p/b, t/d,* etc. But in fact the philosophy behind this method, as presented in the introduction to Chomsky's *Pisa Lectures* (Chomsky 1981), is for syntax too the real methodological revolution behind generative grammar. The difference between a catalogue and a grid is that in the latter *every* property defined for one member is also defined for *all* the others. So in the end every member is defined only in terms of how it differs from all the others. This is one of the most powerful insights ever: it transformed the way we look at the structure not only of language but also of (potentially) any system—so much so that the term associated with this way of looking at things, "structuralism," is one of the unifying ideas of the twentieth century.

Structuralism fostered and made possible the collection of a huge amount of data, in linguistics and in other fields, revealing unexpected and more perspicuous patterns. Breaking things down into primitive differential elements leads to an original and suprising question: what really exists in the end, the bicycles or the abstract features that generate them?

11 BERTRAND RUSSELL

(born Trelleck, Wales, 1872;
died Penrhyndeudraeth, Wales, 1970)

It is a disgrace to the human race that it should have chosen to use the same word "is" for two completely distinct ideas.

—Russell, *Introduction to Mathematical Philosophy*

London, 1918. An inmate of overcrowded Brixton Prison, while the First World War rages outside, Russell finds it in himself to inveigh against a verb. Why such vehemence? What is a frontal attack on the verb "to be" doing in an introduction to mathematics? We have already seen, in the snapshot of Aristotle, that the story of the interpretation of this verb is a very long one. It was analyzed in classical Greece and in medieval treatises, where Abelard coined the term "copula"; it takes on a central role in the baroque period behind the walls of the abbey at Port-Royal; and finally it appears again in the battered notebooks of a prisoner who is trying to rebuild mathematics from the ground up.

The "Homeric Question"—the way the question of the authorship of the *Iliad* and the *Odyssey* has been approached and "solved" in different places and at different times—is a kind of golden thread. If we follow it we can find the key to our civilization, getting a representative general picture of the culture on the basis of how a single question is treated. I think that the story of the interpretation of the verb "to be" has a good case for being considered the "Homeric Question of Linguistics": it leads to a good picture of the nature of thought on language at a particular time or place, with the obvious limitation that, for languages where there is no verb "to be," the thread is broken—but then again, not even Homer is part of every culture. Let us be clear that here we are talking about the verb "to be," not the notion of "being." For those who like labels, we are not making *ontological* observations (from the present participle of the verb "to be" in Ancient Greek: *óntos*) but—to coin a neologism—*einaiological* observations (from the infinitive of the verb "to be" in Ancient Greek: *eínai*). Concerning the motive for using this verb for this concept, I don't think there's anything very mysterious: just as the verb "to do," which is used to identify the class of all possible acts (do a calculation, do a dance, do a somersault, etc.), is really a kind of "pronominal verb" expressing actions in general, "to be," being obligatorily accompanied by a predicate, is that "pronominal verb" which indicates all possible subjects, and so comes to be used to express substance in general—that which exists underneath all properties.

Coming back to Russell, this is a typical example that shows how logic, language, and mathematics have often been treated as facets of a single thing—not always correctly, and not always even coherently. The two ideas that according to Russell are expressed in the same verb are, on the one hand, the attribution of a property to a subject (i.e., predication) and, on the other hand, an identity statement between two individuals. Russell illustrates this allegedly disgraceful situation with two examples: in "Socrates is human"—he says—the verb "to be" signals predication; in "Socrates is a man," on the other hand, it signals identity between two individuals (Socrates and a man). This is the reason for the disgrace, but also the basis of his solution. For a linguist reading the whole passage from Russell, including these examples, a small amount of thought suffices to allay these worries: the "is" of "Socrates is a man" has none of the properties of a verb that involves two individuals, i.e., a transitive verb, for example, "know" in "Socrates knows a man." This can be shown in several ways, for example, by using pronouns and possessive adjectives (the adjectival forms of pronouns). Consider for example a sentence like "Socrates knows an admirer of his:" the sentence is ambiguous: "his" can refer to either Pericles or Socrates. But if I say "Socrates is an admirer of his," "his" cannot refer to Socrates; in this way the verb "to be" differs from all transitive verbs. We could support this conclusion by listing plenty of other properties (see Moro 1997), but what we are interested in now is why Russell got so worked up about this verb: in fact, his concerns reveal a view of language that is quite unexpected.

Everything goes back to the titanic project that Russell was working on in those years: to close the devastating crack that had opened up in the enterprise of basing all of mathematics on logic. This crack, which had in fact been opened up by Russell himself, can be thought of as a monster, a logical monster: the set of all sets that do not contain themselves. Work it out for yourself: there's nowhere to put this set. If the set contains itself, then the definition of the set is wrong, but it can't not contain itself, because then by definition it ought to contain itself, and we're back to square one. Russell found only one way to escape from this monster: to prevent it from being born, by axiomatically ruling out any structure where an element of a given type is attributed a property expressed by elements of the same type. Thus, the monster is aborted. It's a high price, but it has to be paid. This is why Russell was so worried about the verb "to be": he had to avoid assigning a forbidden logical form to sentences like "Socrates is a man," in which an entity of the individual type (Socrates) is attributed a property expressed by the same type: an individual (a man). Putting things this way, there's only one way out: saying that "a man" isn't just a property, but another individual. And so in this case the verb "to be" must necessarily be a predicate, expressing identity (between two individuals), otherwise the sentence would lack one. Hence Russell's despair at the irreducible ambiguity of this verb, an ambiguity that Russell created himself by sticking doggedly to the idea that natural language has a therapeutic relation to logic. As counterevidence, we can point to the anomalous behavior of pronouns when the verb "to be" takes a true predicate of identity, like "identical to." In this case, the behavior of pronouns changes completely, and it becomes similar again to when the predicate is a transitive verb, as in, for example, "Socrates is identical to one of his admirers," where obviously "his" can easily refer to Socrates.

Unfortunately, however, this quotation from Russell has been handed down the generations, and the idea has been uncritically accepted by practically all linguists and philosophers, causing enormous damage, in syntax at least. The only linguist to have realized this seems to have been Otto Jespersen, who criticized the idea bitterly in the first half of the twentieth century, but with little result. When talking about the verb "to be," moreover, there are many interpretative traps that one has to avoid. I hope to have dodged the most dangerous ones when I tried to show how, by applying the techniques of formal linguistics, this supposed disgrace (*at least* this one) disappears like the night before the dawn, and the verb "to be" ends up playing substantially the role that Aristotle suggested: that of "naming the tense."

All the other properties follow from the syntactic structure of the sentence, on the condition that we adopt a rigorous formal framework. The true anomaly lies in the fact that when the verb "to be" is present, the role of predicate can be played by that very category which typically has the subject role (that is, the noun and its dependents, technically referred to as the "noun phrase") as in, for example, "the cause of the riot" in the sentence "A picture of the wall was the cause of the riot." This innocuous-seeming anomaly leads to many surprising facts, for example, that alongside this sentence there's another that appears to be symmetrical to it, as in "The cause of the riot was a picture of the wall," but where the canonical order of grammatical functions is inverse: the predicative noun phrase precedes the copula, whereas the subject follows it. To show that this is a genuine anomaly and that the noun phrase that follows the copula is a subject, it suffices to compare the two following sentences: "Which riot was a picture of the wall the cause of?" and "Which wall was the cause of the riot a picture of?" The latter sentence is hardly grammatical, contrasting with the former: in fact, it is as bad as in the well-known case study exemplified by a sentence like "Which wall does John think that a picture of scared me?" showing that the noun phrase "a picture of the wall" is playing the same role in both ungrammatical sentences, namely that of subject. This anomaly poses a major challenge to the general theory of clause structure, requiring a radical revision along the lines suggested in Moro (1997, 2010); in particular, the canonical enduring interpretation of "subject–predicate" structure assigned to the sequence of a noun phrase and a verb phrase must be abandoned in favor of a more flexible one where the subject is embedded in the verb phrase and the predicate occupies the position normally assigned to the subject.

All of this shouldn't surprise us too much. More often than thought, it's the small and simple anomalies that destabilize apparently solid edifices, and, as Lucretius said, they "open up a trail" toward knowledge of great things (*De rerum natura*, II, 123–24). At least for me, this would never be a disgrace. On the other hand, the shortsightedness that creates the illusion of solidity would be.

12 MARTIN JOOS

(born Wisconsin 1907; died Madison 1978)

Languages can differ from one another unpredictably and without limit.
—Hamp, Joos, Householder, and Austerlitz, eds., *Readings in Linguistics*

Bad luck is sometimes invited. In the sciences, this happens whenever a match, or rather a championship, is declared over. For example, toward the end of the nineteenth century, all that was left for physics was to refine the values of certain natural constants to more decimal places. A few years later, the same models were about as useful as a sundial at night. Relativity and quantum mechanics changed everything. General relativity didn't destroy Newton's theory of gravity, but it demoted it to a special case of a more general theory. Bold assertions of this kind aren't really appropriate in science, although it's difficult to avoid them once you get really involved. A similar fate was in store for this quotation from Joos, only here Fortune was even more brazen, in that in exactly the same year a slim volume was published that was to change the way we see language and take linguistics in exactly the opposite direction: Noam Chomsky's *Syntactic Structures*. In this little book—a summary of a much greater body of work, Chomsky's doctoral thesis, which was only published twenty-five years later (Chomsky 1975)—essentially three points were made. First, linguistic theory should be subjected to the same methodological criteria as any other science; that is, it should proceed on an empirical, not a deductive, basis. Second, the rules for combining words (syntax) could not be captured in terms of statistics, but more sophisticated mathematical tools were needed that took into account long-distance relations between words and brought natural languages under a much more general hierarchy of grammars (Hopcroft et al. 2006). Third, these tools were too complex to be spontaneously learned by children, especially given the relative lack of errors made by children, and above all, the fact that those errors tend to all be of the same type. Actually, this last point wasn't made in the book in question, but rather in an article published two years later, in which Chomsky openly claimed that "The fact that all normal children acquire essentially comparable grammar of great complexity with remarkable rapidity suggests that human beings are somehow specially designed to do this, with data-handling or 'hypothesis-formulating' ability of unknown character and complexity" (Chomsky 1959).

If we think that the complexity of language reflects a blueprint for language, then that blueprint must be the same for everyone. Nobody would think that, for example, there's a genetic blueprint for the structure of the human eye and claim at the same time that the eye can differ substantially from one individual to the next. Of course there are individual or ethnic differences in eyes (for example, the color of the iris or the shape of the eyelid), and group differences (for example, the form of the eyelid), but nobody would say that eyes can vary "unpredictably and without limits."

Thus Joos got it spectacularly wrong. But he couldn't have known, and it would be unfair to dismiss him or make fun of him, and not just for reasons of academic etiquette. Joos's quotation captures a fact that certainly fits with our experience: languages *really do* appear to be completely different from one another. So Joos's quotation doesn't seem at all crazy, just as it doesn't seem crazy to say that the sun orbits the earth. The intuition behind it remains interesting, and it can be reformulated more accurately as follows, with a small but crucial correction: "languages *appear* to differ from one another unpredictably and without limit." In fact, we can go further and point out that in most cases this apparently irreducible variation is associated with mutual unintelligibility, even in relatively small geographical areas. Joos's thought, although mistaken, thus leads us to a genuinely interesting question: why does this "Babel effect" exist?

Here, as often happens, we can't even be sure that there's an answer, because the question is vague and probably misformulated. In biology, for example, it doesn't make sense to ask why there are so many living species—Noah's Babel—if what we want to know is why dragonflies and pigs exist. However, it does make sense to ask why it is *possible* for dragonflies and pigs to exist, and whether there could be "intermediate" animals, part dragonfly and part pig. In this sense, perhaps we can ask what it is that makes the existence of different languages possible, and what the limits to variation are—what, if any, are the limits to Babel? And in fact the goal of much research in contemporary linguistics is exactly to reach a general classification of possible languages, languages that can be spontaneously acquired by children. But, more than this, the question offers an interesting opportunity to think about the commonplace idea that Babel was a curse, all the more interesting today, when international communication is a vital necessity for everyone. In fact, we can think about the *effects* of Babel, and ask ourselves how the world would have turned out if humans had spoken just one language, or if all languages had been mutually intelligible. Let's imagine our world then, in prehistoric times, when building roads, aqueducts, and sewers and simply assuring a food supply were extremely difficult tasks. What would that world have been like if everyone had understood each other and tried to live in the same city—if there had been no "barbarians"? Perhaps humanity would have been ungovernable, and so perhaps language barriers had a protective effect, as epidemics can for different groups of animals in the wild, or apoptosis (programmed cell death) in colonies of cells. Perhaps Babel, in the end, was a gift.

13 ROMAN JAKOBSON

(born Moscow 1906; died Boston 1982)

The break-up of the sound system in aphasics corresponds to the exact mirror image of the development of the phonological system in child language.
—Jakobson, *Kindersprache, Aphasie und allgemeine Lautgesetze*

It sometimes turns out that mistaken discoveries are nonetheless very useful. After all, Columbus never got to India, but the idea of going beyond the limits of the known world and creating new routes, new methods of navigation, and discovering new worlds changed maritime navigation and the map of the planet. In addition to being a striking case of empirical serendipity, the Jakobson quotation is one of the typical opening gambits of aphasiology textbooks. Jakobson is saying that, just as child language acquisition gives us a unique window on the structure of language, language loss in aphasics gives us the opposite perspective, but nonetheless every bit as valid. With hindsight, we can see that the error lay in taking the latest structures to be acquired, thought to be the most difficult to produce, as the first to go, for the same reason. Jakobson came to this conclusion on the basis of phonological phenomena. We all know that children learn certain sounds earlier than others, which is why they seem to muddle "Muggles" and "muddles." But even though this specific model turned out to be false, the method opened up a new, very powerful approach to understanding language: the progressive damage suffered by aphasics gives a unique opportunity to understand the underlying architecture. To use a famous analogy, it is like finding a crack in a marble statue: the natural grain of the rock it was sculpted from is revealed, and so, in the end, are the conditions under which the sculptor produced the final image. So far, nothing unusual. The problem is that in order to understand what has been destroyed, we need to have at least an idea of what *could* be destroyed. So we have to proceed in a two-track fashion, using both clinical observations and linguistic theory. If either is lacking, we will inevitably get derailed. Jakobson again: "Each description and classification of aphasic syndromes must start from the question of which aspects of language are damaged."

A really striking case of an interpretative error was an announcement in the 1990s that (for a while) caused great excitement in certain circles, above all those where being in the spotlight counts for more than being published in a scientific journal. It had been discovered that some members of a family living the London area were unable to form plurals, as in "books" from "book." The distribution of the instances of this deficit in the family tree was surprising: it followed the laws of Mendelian genetics. The newspapers were suddenly full of headlines along the lines of "Grammar Gene Discovered," and in the end a gene really was discovered, by the name of FOXP2. This is indeed a very interesting gene, but it has nothing to do with grammar, leaving syntax aside. Its role is relatively modest and, from the point of view of linguistics, surely peripheral: it contributes to the modulation of fine motor abilities, which among other things are involved in the articulation of sibilants, which are involved in the formation of regular English plurals, written as –s. The media enthusiasm died down, although the discovery was interesting. The story went cold, and instead of talking about a "grammar gene" people started talking about a "speech gene," because the difficulty had nothing to do with plurals but with producing the sound that indicates plurals in English (Fisher and Marcus 2005).

We are still hoping, in a manner of speaking, for a genuine case of grammatical, or perhaps even syntactic, deficit that will carry linguistics triumphantly into the domain of genetics; that is, we are hoping for the birth of "Mendelian linguistics." However, as Peter Medawar has pointed out, the fact that a trait is hereditary doesn't so much mean that it will be expressed in *every* individual in a population but that there will be some individual that does *not* express it (leaving aside evidence coming from direct genetic manipulation, of course).[1] The problem is that syntax, which as we know is the property distinguishing our communication system from those of all other species, doesn't seem to get damaged in the ways we might expect (always assuming that it gets damaged at all). We might in fact ask ourselves whether syntax is like the Kanisza triangle: the illusion of a triangle formed by taking a same-sized segment out of each of three circles and putting them facing each other on a flat surface in just the right way. Perhaps syntax is like that, perhaps the brain perceives it as a unitary object while in fact it isn't one: syntax could be put together and filled in by the brain in ways that we still know nothing about, as a kind of "cognitive optical illusion" (Moro 2008). Perhaps that is why it doesn't get damaged. Does this mean that there is no genetic basis for syntax? Not at all: it probably means that language is determined by the *whole* genetic blueprint for the birth and development of a human being, or perhaps that the genes that express language are also expressed in vital organs following their pleiotropic nature (Hartwell et al. 2015): without them no individual can exist. In other words, our species is somehow protected in its most striking features, for there can exist no human mutants lacking language.

We can thus reaffirm and refine from a genetic perspective a conclusion that we have already reached several times on the basis of different ideas and different data: that language is us, the whole of us all.

14 JOSEPH GREENBERG

(born New York 1915; died Stanford 2001)

With far greater than chance frequency, in a language with the normal order subject-object-verb, the preposition follows the noun.

—Greenberg, Universal 4, from *Universals of Language*

Can we really be sure that science can always trace effects back to their causes? It certainly tries to do that. Descartes wanted to explain the attraction among heavenly bodies in terms of the central dogma of his physics, that in the last analysis all phenomena were due to a chain of mechanical contacts, a domino effect on a cosmic scale. What keeps the Moon in its orbit around the Earth? In order to be consistent with his dogma, Descartes could only hypothesize that there were particles of some invisible substance—the ether—between the Moon and the Earth, and that a huge vortex whose fulcrum is the Earth imprisoned the Moon. Everything fits together very nicely. Pity it's all wrong. Neither the vortex nor the ether exists, not even the ether through which light was supposed to propagate. This latter fact was established by Michelson and Morley, in a famous experiment that led to Einstein's special theory of relativity; they showed that assuming the existence of the ether made things too complicated and forced us into ad hoc explanations. In fact, one of the most astonishing leaps forward in physics happened when Newton was led to give up (temporarily) on the idea of finding a mechanical explanation for gravity, as he states explicitly in his letter to Richard Bentley of February 22, 1692. His famous formula of the attraction between two bodies being inversely proportional to the square of the distance between them and directly proportional to the product of their masses doesn't, in fact, *explain* gravity, unlike the theory of vortices, but provides a reliable description of it, where "reliable" means that predictions can be made on the basis of it, and new questions can be formulated. How can we evaluate a scientific theory other than on the basis of these two properties? Newton certainly ran a great risk in doing what he did; so much so that Leibniz, an orthodox Cartesian, stated quite unambiguously that Newton was dabbling in occult forces in admitting action at a distance (Alexander 1956, Westfall 1983). None of this is of direct interest here; what is of interest is the fact that science can make great progress by giving up on explanation and just trying to describe things. We might almost suspect that science *always* describes and *never* explains, but really that doesn't matter: we've just seen that what really matters is the ability to make predictions and formulate new questions. Let's go back to language, keeping that idea firmly in mind.

With his list of just under fifty universals, among them the one quoted above, Greenberg described certain regularities, but he didn't explain them. In a list of heterogeneous propositions he captured a hidden interplay among apparently independent phenomena. Should we conclude that typological linguistics, the result of this method, is an inferior kind of linguistics? Obviously not: as in the case of Newton, there are times when it's best to leave explanation to one side and proceed by describing (without looking for causes). Often if we don't get any further than this "descriptive" phase it's because we don't really have an idea of the elements that might constitute an explanation: other than by admitting that science can *only* describe. There is another criterion, however, that makes its possible to compare one explanation with another, based neither on the ability to make predictions nor on the ability to formulate new questions, but rather on simplicity: that is, the ability to predict the same phenomena on the basis of the smallest possible number of principles. Lucretius gives us an unsurpassed example (*De rerum Natura*, II, 184–205): in opposition to Aristotelian physics (which had pre-Socratic roots), he said clearly that there's no need to admit the existence of a force that causes certain things to rise (air and fire) and an opposing force that causes certain things to fall (water and earth). We only need a single force that causes things to fall, on the condition that we take the relative density of things into account. For example, a ball filled with cold air will fall in a warm room but will rise from the bottom of a pool of water. We all intuitively recognize that this is a better explanation than one that posits two distinct forces. So (sometimes) the search for simplicity leads to scientific progress; and of course the same is true in linguistics.

Some of Greenberg's universals, certainly Universal 4, can be explained by relatively simple theories if we assume a more abstract representation of linguistic data, as in various models developed starting from an idea of Chomsky's (Graffi 2001). I should add that "abstract" doesn't seem a good term to me: as I understand it, it can only mean "not directly observable by the senses." But if this is what the term means, then it doesn't mean much, if we accept the reasonable methodological assumption put forward in the 1920s by Jean Perrin, according to which "coherent hypotheses concerning what remains invisible can increase our knowledge of what is visible" (Perrin 1913). This principle was formulated for physics, but it's fully applicable to linguistics, provided that an equivalent of "visible" is adopted. It would be tempting to conclude that perhaps everything that exists is just what contributes to explanation.

In the end it's like looking at the back of a tapestry and realizing that the patches of color that appear on the other side, forming such elaborate pictures, are nothing other than threads sewn in and out of the cloth in such a way as to form unexpected connections between different parts of the design. The back of the verbal tapestry, the hidden warp and weft that gives rise to the structure, is perhaps all we can expect of explanations in linguistics.

15 ERIC H. LENNEBERG

(born Düsseldorf 1921;
died White Plains, N.Y., 1975)

Biological research on language seems to be paradoxical to the extent
that we have to acknowledge that languages consist of arbitrary cultural
constraints. —Lenneberg, *Biological Foundations of Language*

Ideology is science's worst enemy. It creates expectations of data, makes
the nonexistent seem real, and in the end leads straight to bitter disap-
pointment. In *Life and Destiny* Vassily Grossman prepares the reader
for the systematic and perverse annihilation of humanity by totalitarian
regimes in his description of how the roads, railways, and power lines of
the Nazi concentration camp imprison everything with their geometric
rigor: "It was a space filled with straight lines; a space of rectangles and
parallelograms that cut through the foggy autumn sky." If we don't take
into account the rough-edged and irreducible facts, if we let ideology
prevail over data, we risk paralysis. This was where linguistics was in the
mid-twentieth century: through a desire to impose at all costs the notion

that languages are "arbitrary cultural conventions," work on the biology of language was effectively ruled out.

In his treatise on the biological foundations of language, Eric Lenneberg felt obliged to include this prefatory caveat. Was this really necessary? It wouldn't be today, thanks to the fact that Lenneberg concluded his work by demonstrating that recovery from aphasia, if it was possible, had different outcomes depending on whether the lesion happened before or after puberty. If the lesion had been before puberty, then the chances of recovery were better, and, tellingly, recovering patients tended to follow the same developmental path as children acquiring language spontaneously. If the lesion was postpuberty, patients tended to recover less, and the recovery typically followed a chaotic path. Language acquisition is thus sensitive to a so-called "critical period" in which latent abilities are either stimulated or lost, as is well known to be the case with many other biological phenomena we understand much better because they can be studied in animals. Now it would certainly seem strange to say that the age of puberty was an "arbitrary cultural convention" (although of course it can vary as a function of complex variables to do with nutrition and social factors), so the idea that language in general is an arbitrary convention becomes somewhat implausible.

However, Lenneberg's quotation cannot be put aside so easily. English usage sets a trap (which can be avoided in various other languages, including Italian), since we use a single word, "language," for both specific tongues and language in general (where Italian, for example, uses *lingua* in the first sense and *linguaggio* in the second). In English the two senses are only distinguished in the plural, so we interpret Lenneberg to mean that research on *language* in general appears to be paradoxical because individual *languages* must be taken to be arbitrary cultural conventions. This is the fundamental point and the real novelty in relation to the nineteenth-century research tradition that continued into the latter part of the twentieth century (Bambini 2012): the new, central question is not the extent to which *language in general*, in the sense of the capacity to communicate, depends on the brain (this is considered to be firmly entrenched) but if the *structure of human language* does, that is, whether *particular languages*, and in particular their syntax, do (since syntax marks the watershed between the human communication system and those of other animals).

Despite that fact that ideological prejudices are never satisfied but rather tend to become more disingenuous, since they admit that science is something more than a method (the opium of the people, perhaps), the results are encouraging. Among the most solidly confirmed results are those obtained from neuroimaging techniques, as long as they don't give way to a tendency toward a new phrenology. I mention this because it's important to underline that this type of research doesn't consist in finding neuropsychological correlates to specific activities in order to produce a functional map of the brain, but rather in understanding how it is possible for the obviously modular structure of the brain to give rise to the cognitive and behavioral activities we observe—a step analogous in certain respects to what happened earlier in linguistics in phonology and then in syntax with the abandonment of taxonomies in favor of decomposition of units into more primitive elements. The other risk, of course, consists in translating the formal generalizations of linguistics into neuronal mechanisms: this is a premature goal, and it's not even clear that it can ever be reached without radically changing our ideas about neuronal mechanisms. On the other hand, what we can do and what is in fact being done is to check whether certain very general properties of the structure of language discovered by formal approaches are reflected in dedicated neural networks. In this area, as I said above, the results are encouraging. It has been shown that the brain is not at all neutral to the type of grammar it is exposed to. For example, if exposed to a syntax without recursive rules, the activity of the language circuits diminishes gradually in favor of other circuits that are typically implicated in solving nonlinguistic problems. But this tells us nothing about the neuropsychological algorithms working at the level of neuronal mechanisms that make this distinction possible (Moro et al. 2001; Tettamanti et al. 2002, 2008b; Musso et al. 2005; Friederici et al. 2006; Moro 2013, 2015; Dehaene et al. 2015). The old idea that the brain is hardware that runs various kinds of software—grammars, but also other cognitive capacities—is thus completely outmoded (Di Francesco 2002): software—i.e., the grammars of different languages—is really to be thought of as an expression of the hardware, determining its structural limits.

The limits to Babel thus exist and are inscribed in our bodies. Obviously, that doesn't mean that we'll manage to *reduce* language comprehension to neurological mechanisms (an idea that I personally do not even understand); but we might be able to see the extent to which neurological mechanisms are isomorphic to the structures of natural language (see Poepple 1996; Moro 2015; Dehaene et al. 2015 and references cited there), if at all, and consequently to define and circumscribe the limits to variations of these mechanisms, in order to be able to define, on neurobiological grounds, the class of possible languages. In other words, we could arrive at a "rational anatomy" of grammar. This is certainly not much, perhaps nothing at all, in relation to all that the totality of language means to us humans: poetry, curses, promises, prayers, sweet nothings, and jokes all fall outside of this project. But there are no reasonable alternatives.

It's as if we were in the position of someone who, asked to define a caress, could only describe the structure of the hand and the angles of rotation of the bones, muscles, and tendons that constitute it: it wouldn't be easy to distinguish it from a slap. But if nothing else, at least it wouldn't be confused with a kick, and that's a start.

16 NIELS JERNE

(born London 1911; died Castillon-du-Gard 1994)

> I find it astonishing that the immune system has a degree of complexity
> that suggests parallels, more or less superficial but nonetheless surpris-
> ing, with human language.
>
> —Jerne, *The Generative Grammar of the Immune System*

Who would ever have thought that when I sneeze in someone's face and
when I say something to them, their body, in a certain sense, reacts in the
same way? To be more precise, the way the information contained in a
sneeze is recognized is not dissimilar from the way the information contained in a sentence is recognized. The body—whether it's the brain or
the lymphatic system—must recognize that it's dealing with something
distinct from itself, that comes from somewhere else, otherwise there will
be problems. If I considered a sentence that I hear as if I had said it, or a
sentence that comes to my mind as if someone had said it, then I wouldn't
be able to understand anything about myself or about the world. In the
same way, my immune system must be able to distinguish what belongs
to me from what doesn't belong to me in order to know whether to attack

it, digest it, or leave it alone. Jerne's extraordinary discovery, which earned him the Nobel Prize for Medicine or Physiology, was that the immune system is not formed *solely* on the spur of the moment as a reaction to the outside world, but that there is a superabundant repertoire of antibodies that exists prior to experience, which the organism can apply when it comes into contact with antigens such as viruses and bacteria (see Paul 2013). In the same way, when a sentence enters the brain the system that deciphers it isn't formed just as a reaction to that sentence: there is a superabundant repertoire that exists prior to experience, which the brain applies when it comes in contact with a linguistic code. This is the essential idea behind what is known as "Universal Grammar": part of our ability to understand language is based on something that *precedes* experience, exactly as in the case of the immune system. Looking at things from a more speculative perspective, we can say that Universal Grammar is nothing other than a theory of the limits of experience in determining the development of the linguistic code. In essence, generative grammar captures the individual human's "linguistic brain stem."

But if we are to take this theory seriously, what other features would we expect the structure of language to have? There's one that seems particularly telling. We know that all human languages have recursive syntax: as we have seen, this implies that there are no rules in any natural language that can relate two words at a fixed distance, not even the first and last words of a sentence. We also know that if we try to teach the brain a nonrecursive syntax, it can learn it, but the language circuits are progressively disengaged (see Moro 2013, 2015 and the references given there). What has all this got to do with the biological question? Because in a certain sense it's like what happened when Europeans first reached America, exporting, among other things, bacteria and viruses to which the indigenous populations had no resistance (Oldstone 1998). Their immune systems, sensitive to local pathogens, couldn't react. Fortunately, sentences don't have such devastating effects, and if someone speaks to us using a nonrecursive syntax we don't fall ill. But this isn't the point. The point is that nature doesn't give organisms unlimited time to adapt, nor is it disposed to alter a work in progress (or at least almost never): it is very rare for an organism to face new conditions by restructuring some part of itself, other than at the microscopic level, as in the case of a scar. It would be a little like changing the wings of an aircraft in flight: both difficult and dangerous. The modifications a human can make to itself are, generally speaking, purely microscopic. However, there are some unexpected exceptions, teeth, for example: at a certain point the first useful variant falls out and is substituted by another. But this isn't because the old ones were worn out, so much so that it doesn't happen for other organs that are much more heavily used: we have milk teeth, but not "milk eyes" or a "milk liver," nor do we have "milk syntax." There's no simple explanation for this peculiarity of teeth. But, to keep to the cognitive domain, it would be very advantageous if adults could spontaneously learn more efficient and powerful possibly infinite syntaxes. But this doesn't happen, just as we don't learn to drink untreated sea water, even though that would be extremely useful for the survival of our species.

Perhaps there is a reason adults only use recursive syntax, but it simply can't be reconstructed either from the phylogenetic history of the species or from the ontogenetic history of the individual (Moro 2011b)—a situation comparable to that of a future archaeologist who finds computer keyboards but not typewriters. That archaeologist would never imagine that the current layout of the keys wasn't designed, as it would be natural to think, in order to facilitate the association between the most frequent letters and the easiest fingers to move, but rather by the need (which these days for purely technological reasons no longer holds) to prevent, as far as possible, the type bars corresponding to the most frequent English letters from getting in each other's way: in fact, the "qwerty" arrangement is one of the possible solutions to a technological problem. The cost was that the layout of the keys looks chaotic (at least in relation to the universally accepted and ubiquitous alphabetical order), but the practical advantage won out: this layout reduces the need to stop to untangle the type bars (Liebowitz & Margolis 1990). Perhaps, then, the recursive structure that we find in today's syntax might have been advantageous for some ontogenetic or phylogenetic reason that has now vanished, and hence it seems to us groundless. Perhaps this structure is useless now, even counterproductive, but it would be too costly to introduce a "milk syntax" into our genetic blueprint.

Perhaps. But what is certain is that we are born with a kind of biological sieve that, prior to experience, limits the number of attainable grammars from the start. And this is a great help to language acquisition. Otherwise it would be like having to have every possible kind of cold before being able to get better from one.

17 NOAM CHOMSKY

(born Philadelphia 1928)

Language is more like a snowflake than a giraffe's neck. Its specific properties are determined by laws of nature, they have not developed through the accumulation of historical accidents.

—Chomsky (2004), extrapolation and adaptation of the text agreed with the author; see also J. Russell (2004)

This is not a group photo. This is a portrait of an individual who, despite appearances, is somewhat isolated. It's an unexpectedly difficult photo, one of those that make you realize that the journey isn't yet over. At least three preliminary points should be made before we can understand it.

The first is a logical deduction: if the distinctive characteristic of human language is syntax, and if the distinctive characteristic of syntax is recursion—i.e., the capacity to produce potentially infinite hierarchical structures (by iterating basic operations)—there *cannot* be any precursors to language either in the phylogenetic or in the ontogenetic sense. Given this definition, in fact, syntax is an all-or-nothing affair: it's either there or it isn't. Saying that it is partly there, or that it can be approximated in stages, would be like saying that there's a number big enough that when you add it to another number it gives infinity—a mathematical mirage—or that there could be a precursor of arithmetic that works only up to a certain number. The second point is a comparative one: the syntactic structure of human languages has no equivalents in the communication systems of any other living creature. As we saw above, this has been known since Descartes' time. What's new is that we can now specify the nature of the structural difference in mathematical terms, rather than intuitively, anecdotally, or metaphorically. That structural difference involves "recursion" (and all rules, including locality, are based on it). The third preliminary is experimental: we know that when we generate or interpret a sentence constructed using recursive syntax, a particular set of neural networks are activated, which are *not* activated or, more precisely, progressively disengaged, in the case of "impossible grammars," using nonrecursive syntax. This is a robust result, which has been reproduced in numerous experiments at different research centers around the world (see Kaan & Swaab 2002; Marcus et al. 2003; Monti et al. 2009; Moro 2013, 2015; Friederici et al. 2006; Cappa 2012; Dehaene et al. 2015). It rules out the possibility of taking syntax to be an "arbitrary cultural convention," which worried Lenneberg. Physiology is not a matter of convention.

It's not hard to see that these points are not easily reconciled with one another. On the one hand, the syntax of human languages must appear *en bloc*; on the other hand, the brain, the organ that expresses it, can only be the result of a gradual process of evolution. Of course, evolution can show sudden accelerations alternating with periods of stasis (as put forward in Gould's theory of punctuated equilibrium), but aside from the rate of change, everything necessarily happens step by step. In a famous letter, Darwin himself warns against making exceptions in this connection (cited in Gould 2002): "If it could be shown that there exists a complex organ which *cannot* be formed by numerous small successive modifications, my theory would certainly collapse." In the course of evolution there have been cases where a structure appeared in an organism suddenly (so to speak), but preformed structures were imported from outside the organism, as in the well-known case of the importation of an archeobacterium into eukaryotic cells as a precursor to mitochondria. Even if we were to say something analogous about human language, the only outcome would be to displace the question of the origin of this structure.

We are led to a paradoxical conclusion: the structure of language does not obey the biological laws that have given rise to the neurobiological structure that expresses it, the brain. After all, only we humans have this structure, which leads us to exclude the possibility that the selective pressure giving rise to it came from the need to communicate, unless of course we deny that we are the only living species whose language has this type of syntax.

From this strange and simultaneously fascinating perspective, we can see the importance of Chomsky's suggestion that the structure of language is more like a snowflake than a giraffe's neck. Each snowflake, among innumerable but not infinite variations, represents, in a sense, one possible "solution" to a complicated physical equation: its structure is an almost instantaneous response to the conditions of temperature, gravity, air pressure, quantity and purity of water, etc. The structure of language might be formed in the same way: an instantaneous solution that satisfies independent conditions whose nature and complexity escape us. As for the differences among languages, individual languages might be the expression of the degrees of freedom allowed by the system, like the differences among snowflakes. Of course, I'm talking about the structure of language here, not about the brain: the brain is the result of a process that is anything but instantaneous, in which chance and history play a role, just as they do in the case of the giraffe's neck.

It's not at all easy to imagine a theory that brings together these two connected but apparently irreconcilable phenomena: it's possible that we'll never come up with one, or that we'll do it only by radically transforming neurobiology, much as Newton radically transformed the contemporary dominant Cartesian models of physics. Besides, even though today our knowledge of the relevant phenomena is incomparably more detailed than in the past, this *impasse* has ancient roots, as we have seen. Not even Descartes managed to reconcile the unique, "rational," and creative in human language with a material basis as required by the mechanistic dogma, and so was led to his famous dualistic philosophy, hypothesizing two distinct and irreducible levels of reality: "the stuff of thought" (*res cogitans*) and "the stuff that occupies space" (*res extensa*). We've also seen that the much more recent idea of assimilating the brain to hardware and language to software is also no help. We shouldn't exclude the possibility, then, if every attempt at reduction to some other level of organization fails, that it might be better to hypothesize (at least temporarily) a level of organization whose characteristics are derived neither from neurobiology nor from formal properties. We could call this "mindware." Doing this, we would be close to Newton's approach when he (temporarily) admitted the possibility of action at a distance as an explanatory part of the theory of gravity. Besides, the only thing that counts in science is being able to make predictions and formulate new questions.

In all this irreducible uncertainty, there's just one thing I'm sure of: the human brain is a unique object in the biological world. The combination of two independent properties attests to this: the fact that the recursive structure of human language has no counterparts in other species, and the fact that this recursive structure is an expression of the brain, in fact the only possible one in the case of language, and not an "arbitrary cultural convention." Whatever conclusion you want to draw from these facts, and here anybody's opinion is as valid as anyone else's, I think that the famous conclusion to Jacques Monod's book *Chance and Necessity* (Monod 1970, Newman 1973) does not necessarily hold. Where he says, "The ancient illusion has been destroyed: we humans know that we stand alone in the indifferent immensity of a Universe from which we emerged by chance. Neither our duty nor our destiny are written anywhere. The choice between the Kingdom and the Darkness is ours alone," I would just add that, at least for me, choosing chance is rather a step toward the Darkness.

FINALE

The devil doesn't promise you everything; he just makes you think that something is enough.

—Anon.

This is the end of the photo album. If, as sometimes happens with amateur photos, you see me reflected here and there in a mirror or worse, my hand in a picture, I hope you'll forgive me and, above all, that this won't have detracted from the intrinsic interest of the subjects. They are all still there, available for further photos. To tell the truth, innumerable snapshots didn't find their way into this album: those of Nikolai Trubetzkoy, Alfred Tarski, Louis Hjemslev, Leonard Bloomfield, Otto Jespersen, Richard Montague, Richard Kayne, in primis. There's only one person, however, of whom I thought no snapshot would ever be possible: I wouldn't change even a comma of the first seven chapters of the first book of *De vulgari eloquentia*—but I don't have Pierre Menard's calling.

So this album isn't complete, but the real question is whether an album whose subject is language could ever be. Sometimes language seems to slip away from our grasp the way the tortoise did from Achilles: every time we get closer to it, it seems to move a little further away. But it's not in my nature to be discouraged. Perhaps we'll never really catch this tortoise, but I'm convinced that we'll get close enough to look it in the eyes.

POSTSCRIPT

The way I've been talking about language here might give rise to a rather unnatural picture. It's a kind of anatomical sketch, showing a certain amount of detail, but inevitably dry and lifeless. I'm aware of this, and I've tried to point it out explicitly wherever I could. We can only describe the structural limits of language in the individual and in the species, that is, the "boundaries of Babel." But we all perceive language through the creative use and experience of it that each of us has, even in this precise moment. Nobody has the right to decide whether one sentence should be valued above all others: respect for every sentence, and the responsibility that comes with it, arises from the fact that behind every sentence there is a person. Once more, and for the last time, I want to illustrate this with a quotation. It's taken from a book about New York in the 1940s. It doesn't mention language at all; it's about a tree. The fact is that when you really care about something, you end up caring about everything, about the unrepeatable nature of reality and of life in all its forms, a mystery far greater than we are. What follows should give a sense of the idea, and what is true for a tree is true for a sentence.

A block or two west of the new City of Man in Turtle Bay there is an old willow tree that presides over an interior garden. It is a battered tree, long suffering and much climbed, held together by strands of wire but beloved of those who know it. In a way, it symbolizes the city: life under difficulties, growth against odds, sap-rise in the midst of concrete, and a steady reaching for the sun. Whenever I look at it nowadays, and feel the cold shadow of the planes, I think: "This must be saved, this particular thing, this very tree." If it were to go, all would go—this city, this mischievous and marvelous monument which not to look upon would be like death.

ACKNOWLEDGMENTS

When I began this work I didn't anticipate the feeling that came to me at the end: I realized that talking about these figures had made me feel I was part of a group. The people pictured—aside from God, of course—look at each other across the pages, they smile at one another or ignore one another, but they're nonetheless a group. Putting together these figures made me realize that the passion I feel when I talk about language, and it is a real passion, is connected to my feeling part of a group. I'm not interested in being a leader, and I'm not one; for me it's enough to participate since, as Giorgio Gaber sang, "freedom is participation."

My thanks also go to the group of friends and teachers who have generously discussed and commented on the ideas in the foregoing pages with me on various occasions: Noam Chomsky, Giorgio Graffi, Luigi Rizzi, Gennaro Chierchia, Massimo Piattelli-Palmarini, Richard Kayne, Giuseppe Longobardi, Edoardo Boncinelli, Stefano Cappa, Marco Tettamanti, Salvatore Veca, Massimo Cacciari, Giuseppe Trautteur, Alessandra Tommaselli, Ken Hale, Valentina Bambini, Marco Riva, Tommaso Bellini, Michele Di Francesco, Rita Manzini, Guido Andreolli, Jacques Mehler, Matteo Greco, Roberto Tintinelli, Pier Marco Bertinetto, Alberto Ferrari, Guglielmo Cinque, Daniela Perani, Stefano Arduini, Maria Elena

Moro, Lorenzo Magrassi, Rosella Testera, Angelo Moro, Umberto Manfredini, Fabio Bonetti, Ersilia Cattaneo, Remigio Allegri, Neil Smith, Ian Roberts, Giulio Lepschy, Giovanni Nava, and Franco Bottoni. Thanks to Matteo Codignola for his faith, encouragement, and patience, which were crucial in putting together this collection, and to my literary agent, Marco Vigevani. The stubborn resistance to all their useful suggestions is all my own work. A special thanks to Eric Schwartz, who followed and fostered the English version with great generosity, intelligence, and patience. I also wish I could find the proper words to thank Ian Roberts, who translated this book: Ian is for me the rare synthesis of a *maestro* and a friend, and this translation was an undeserved and unsolicited present he gave me. The way he interpreted my Italian and resurrected it into his mother tongue is so impressive for me that if it weren't too baroque a path, it should be retranslated into Italian to make it as shining as it is in his own interpretation. Leslie Kriesel, finally, did a wonderful job in intercepting my residual errors. This book is dedicated to anyone who never wanted to write anything.

NOTES

5. ROGER BACON

1. Translator's note: the Latin word for "mirror" is *speculum*.
2. To be more precise, language can live outside our skull in different formats alongside sound waves, such as writing. Indeed, in this case too the sound is organized in waves, the electromagnetic waves of light shaped by writing: whether the writing system is phonologically or ideographically based is a different issue; what is important is that the physical stimulus of writing obviously does not contain acoustic stimuli. Notably, when language is written the linearity requirement is not respected and the entire sequence appears simultaneously, although to read it we can only parse it word by word in a sequence again.

6. DESCARTES

1. See Chomsky (1956, 2012), Kayne (1994, 2011), Moro (2000, 2009).

9. HERMANN OSTHOFF; E. KARL BRUGMANN

1. Chomsky (1975, 2004), Trautteur (2002), Moro (2015).

11. BERTRAND RUSSELL

This snapshot is largely based on Moro (1997, 2010) and all the references given there.

13. ROMAN JAKOBSON

1. Medawar (1967).

BIBLIOGRAPHY

(Where all the works cited and much more can be found, but not God)

Given the nature of this book, I decided that it wasn't a good idea to burden the text with notes and highly specific references. But of course I want to give the references to the principal sources and where the ideas (mine and, above all, others') can be read about in more detail. Some texts have been cited in the foregoing; others are cited here as good sources for learning more about language and related matters. A general introduction to the question of the relation of language to the brain and the special properties of the syntax of human languages is given in Moro (2015); for the source of most of the scientific works of mine I referred to in the text, see Moro (2013); the only one not included there is Magrassi et al. (2015).

Abutalebi, J., S. Brambati, J. M. Annoni, A. Moro, S. Cappa, and D. Perani. 2007. "Auditory Perception of Language Switches: Controlled Versus Automatic Processing as Revealed by Event-Related fMRI." *Journal of Neuroscience* 27 (50): 13762–69.

Akmajian, A., R. A. Demers, A. K. Farmer, and R. M. Harnish. 2010. *Linguistics: An Introduction to Language and Communication*. Cambridge, Mass.: MIT Press.

Alexander, H. G., ed. 1956. *The Leibniz-Clarke Correspondence: Together with Extracts from Newton's Principia and Opticks*. Manchester: Manchester University Press.

Anderson, S. R. 2008. "The Logical Structure of Linguistic Theory: Presidential Address to the Linguistic Society of America Annual Meeting, Chicago, January 5, 2008." *Language* 84: 795–814.

Bambini, V. 2010. "Neuropragmatics: A Foreword." *Italian Journal of Linguistics* 22 (1): 1–20.

——. 2012. "Neurolinguistics." In *Handbook of Pragmatics*, ed. J.-O. Östman and J. Verschueren. Amsterdam: John Benjamins Publishing Company.

Bertinetto, P. M. 1983. *Tempo, aspetto e azione nel verbo italiano: Il sistema dell'indicativo*. Firenze: Accademia della Crusca.

Berwick, R. 1985. *The Acquisition of Syntactic Knowledge*. Cambridge, Mass.: MIT Press.

——. 2009. "What Genes Can't Learn About Language." *PNAS* 106 (6): 1685–86.

——. 2011. "Syntax Facit Saltum Redux: Biolinguistics and the Leap to Syntax." In *The Biolinguistic Enterprise*, ed. A.-M. Di Sciullo and C. Boeck, 65–99. Oxford, New York: Oxford University Press.

Bonomi, A., and A. Zucchi. 2001. *Tempo e linguaggio*. Milano: Bruno Mondadori.

Cacciari, M., M. Donà, and R. Gasparotti. 1987. *Le forme del fare*. Napoli: Liguori.

Calvin, W., and G. Ojemann. 1994. *Conversation with Neil's Brain: The Neural Nature of Thought and Language*. Reading, Mass.: Addison-Wesley.

Cappa, S. 2001. *Cognitive Neurology: An Introduction*. London: Imperial College Press.

——. 2012. "Imaging Semantics and Syntax." *NeuroImage* 61 (2): 427–31. doi:10.1016/j.neuroimage.2011.10.006.

Casalegno, P. 1997. *Filosofa del linguaggio: Un'introduzione*. Rome: Carocci.

Casati, R., and A. C. Varzi. 1994. *Holes and Other Superficialities*. Cambridge, Mass.: MIT Press.

Catani, M., and M. Thiebaut de Schotten. 2012. *Atlas of Human Brain Connections*. Oxford: Oxford University Press.

Céline, L.-F. 1952. *Semmelweis (1818–1865)*. Paris: Gallimard.

Changeux, J.-P., P. Courrège, and A. Danchin. 1973. "A Theory of the Epigenesis of Neuronal Networks by Selective Stabilization of Synapses." *PNAS* 70 (10): 2974–78.

Chierchia, G. 1993. "Logica e linguistica: Il contributo di Montague." In *La filosofia analitica del linguaggio*, ed. M. Santanbrogio, 287–359. Bari: Laterza.

Chierchia, G., and S. McConnell Ginet. 2002. *Meaning and Grammar*. Cambridge, Mass.: MIT Press.

Chomsky, N. 1956. "Three Models for the Description of Grammar." *I.R.E.: Transaction on Information Theory*, IT-2, 113–24. Reprinted in *Readings in Mathematical Psychology, Vol. II.*, ed. R. D. Luce, R.R. Bush, and E. Galanter. New York: Wiley.

——. 1959. Review of Skinner 1957. *Language* 35:26–58.

——. 1975. *The Logical Structure of Linguistic Theory*. Chicago: University of Chicago Press.

——. 1981. *Lectures on Government and Binding*. Dordrecht: Foris.

——. 1993. *Language and Thought*. Wakefeld: Moyer Bell.

——. 2004. *The Generative Enterprise Revisited*. Berlin, New York: Mouton de Gruyter.

——. 2012. "Poverty of the Stimulus: Willingness to Be Puzzled." In *Rich Languages from Poor Inputs*, ed. M. Piattelli Palmarini and R. Berwick. Oxford: Oxford University Press.

——. 2013. "Problems of Projection." *Lingua* 130 (June): 33–49.

Corballis, M. 2003. *From Hand to Mouth: The Origins of Language*. Princeton: Princeton University Press.

De Mauro, T. 2007. *Linguistica elementare*. Bari: Laterza.

Dehaene, S. 1999. *The Number Sense: How the Mind Creates Mathematics*. Oxford: Oxford University Press.

——. 2009. *Reading in the Brain*. New York: Penguin.

Dehaene, S., F. Meynel, C. Wacongne, C. Wang, and C. Pallier. 2015. "The Neural

Representation of Sequences: From Transition Probabilities to Algebraic Patterns and Linguistic Trees." *Neuron* 88 (1): 2–19.

Denes, G. 2009. *Talking Heads: The Neuroscience of Language.* London: Psychology Press.

Derbyshire, J. 2003. *Prime Obsession: Bernhard Riemann and the Greatest Unsolved Problem of Mathematics.* Washington, D.C.: Joseph Henry Press.

Di Francesco, M. 2002. *Introduzione alla filosofia della mente.* Rome: Carocci.

Du Bois-Reymond, E. 1874. "The Limits of Our Knowledge of Nature." *Popular Science Monthly* 5 (May–June): 17–32, 369.

Eco, U. 1993. *La ricerca della lingua perfetta nella cultura europea.* Bari: Laterza.

Feynman, R. 1967. *The Character of the Physical Law.* Cambridge, Mass.: MIT Press.

Fisher, S., and G. Marcus. 2005. "The Eloquent Ape: Genes, Brains and the Evolution of Language." *Nature*, January 7, 9–20.

Friederici, A., J. Bahlmann, S. Heim, R. I. Schubotz, and A. Anwander. 2006. "The Brain Differentiates Human and Non-Human Grammars. Functional Localization and Structural Connectivity." *PNAS* 103:2458–63.

Gould, S. J. 2002. *The Structure of Evolutionary Theory.* Cambridge, Mass.: Belknap Press of Harvard University Press.

Graff, G. 2001. *200 Years of Syntax: A Critical Survey.* Amsterdam: John Benjamins Publishing Company.

———. 2010. *Due secoli di pensiero linguistico.* Rome: Carocci.

Hartwell, L., M. Goldberg, J. Fischer, L. Hood, and C. Aquadro. 2015. *Genetics: From Genes to Genomes.* 5th ed. New York: McGraw-Hill Education.

Hickok, G. 2014. *The Myth of Mirror Neurons: The Real Neuroscience of Communication and Cognition.* New York: Norton.

Hopcroft, J.E., R. Motwani, and J. D. Ullmann. 2006. *Introduction to Automata Theory, Languages, and Computation.* Atlanta: Addison-Wesley.

Kaan, E., and T. Swaab. 2002. "The Brain Circuitry of Syntactic Comprehension." *Trends in Cognitive Science* 6:350–56.

Kandel, E., J. Schwartz, T. Jessell, S. Siegelbaum, and A. Hudspeth. 2012. *Principles of Neural Science.* New York: McGraw-Hill Medical.

Kayne, R. 1994. *The Antisymmetry of Syntax*. Cambridge, Mass.: MIT Press.

——. 2011. "Why Are There No Directionality Parameters?" In *Proceedings of the 28th West Coast Conference on Formal Linguistics*, 1–23. Somerville, Mass.: Cascadilla Proceedings Project.

Kneale, W., and M. Kneale. 1962. *The Development of Logic*. Oxford: Clarendon Press.

Lepschy, G. C., ed. 1990–1994. *Storia della linguistica*. 3 vols. Bologna: il Mulino.

Lesky, A. 1971. *Geschichte der griechischen Literatur*. Bern-München: Francke.

Levi-Montalcini, R. 1987. *In Praise of Imperfection: My Life and Works*. New York: Basic Books.

Liebowitz, S. J., and S. E. Margolis 1990. "The Fable of the Keys." *Journal of Law Economy* 30 (1): 1–26.

Longobardi, G. 2003. "Methods in Parametric Linguistics and Cognitive History." *Linguistic Variation Yearbook* 3:101–38.

Longobardi, G., and I. Roberts. 2010. "Universals, Diversity and Change in the Science of Language: Reaction to *The Myth of Language Universals and Cognitive Science*." *Lingua* 120 (12): 2699–703.

Lucretius, T., and M. Smith. 2001. *On the Nature of Things*. Indianapolis: Hackett.

Magrassi, L., G. Aromataris, A. Cabrini, V. Annovazzi Lodi, and A. Moro. 2015. "Sound Representation in Higher Language Areas During Language Generation." *Proceedings of the National Academy of Science PNAS* 112 (6): 1868–73. Published ahead of print January 26, 2015; doi:10.1073/pnas.1418162112.

Magrassi, L., D. Bongetta, S. Bianchini, M. Berardesca, and C. Arienta. 2010. "Central and Peripheral Components of Writing Critically Depend on a Defined Area of the Dominant Superior Parietal Gyrus." *Brain Research* 1346 (July 30): 145–54.

Manzini, M. R. 1992. *Locality*. Cambridge, Mass.: MIT Press.

Marcus, G., A. Vouloumanos, and I. A. Sag. 2003. "Does Broca's Play by the Rules?" *Nature Neuroscience* 6 (7): 651–52.

Martino, G. 2010. *Identità e mutamento*. Milano: Editrice San Raffaele.

Medawar, P. B. 1967. *The Art of the Soluble*. London: Methuen.

Mehler, J. 1974. "Connaître par désapprentissage." In *L'Unité de l'homme 2. Le cerveau humain*, ed. E. Morin and M. Piattelli Palmarini, 25–37. Paris: Éditions du Seuil.

Monod, J. 1970. *Le Hazard e la nécessité. Essai sur la philosophie naturelle de la biologie modern*. Paris: Éditions du Seuil.

Monti, M., L. Parsons, and D. Osherson. 2009. "The Boundaries of Language and Thought: Neural Basis of Inference Making." *PNAS* 106 (20): 12554–59.

Moro, A. 1997. *The Raising of Predicates*. Cambridge: Cambridge University Press.

——. 2000. *Dynamic Antisymmetry*. Cambridge, Mass.: MIT Press.

Moro, A., M. Tettamanti, D. Perani, C. Donati, S. F. Cappa, and E. Fazio. 2001. "Syntax and the Brain: Disentangling Grammar by Selective Anomalies." *NeuroImage* 13:110–18.

——. 2009. *Rethinking Symmetry: A Note on Labelling and the EPP*. In *La grammatica tra storia e teoria: Scritti in onore di Giorgio Graff*, ed. P. Cotticelli Kurras and A. Tomaselli, 129–31. Alessandria: Edizioni dell'Orso.

——. 2010. *Breve storia del verbo "essere": Viaggio al centro della frase*. Milano: Adelphi.

——. 2011a. "A Closer Look at the Turtle's Eyes." *PNAS* 108 (6): 2177–78.

——. 2011b. "'Kataptation,' or the QWERTY-effect in Language Evolution." *Frontiers in Psychology* 2:50. doi: 10.3389/fpsyg.2011.00050.

——. 2013. *The Equilibrium of Human Syntax: Symmetries in the Brain*. New York: Routledge.

——. 2015. *The Boundaries of Babel: The Brain and the Enigma of Impossible Languages, Second Edition*. Cambridge, Mass.: MIT Press.

Moro, A. Forthcoming. *Impossible Languages*. Cambridge, Mass.: MIT Press.

Musso, M., A. Moro, V. Glauche, M. Rijntjes, J. Reichenbach, C. Büchel, and C. Weiller. 2003. "Broca's Area and the Language Instinct." *Nature Neuroscience* 6:774–81.

Newman, J. 1879. *An Essay in Aid of a Grammar of Assent*. London: Longman.

——. 1973. Letter to J. Walker Scarborough (1868). In *The Letters and Diaries of John Henry Newman*, ed. C. S. Dessain and T. Gornall. Oxford: Clarendon Press, XXIV:77–78.

Newmeyer, F. J. 2005. *Possible and Probable Languages: A Generative Perspective on Linguistic Typology*. Oxford: Oxford University Press.

Oldstone, M. 1998. *Viruses, Plague, and History*. Oxford: Oxford University Press.

Pallier, C., A.-D. Devauchelle, and S. Dehaene. 2011. "Cortical Representation of the Constituent Structure of Sentences." *PNAS* 108:2522–27.

Paul, W., ed. 2013. *Fundamental Immunology*. 7th ed. Philadephia: Wolters Kluwer.

Perrin, J. 1913. *Les Atoms*. Paris: Alcan.

Poeppel, D. 1996. "Neurobiology and Linguistics Are Not Yet Unifiable." *Behavioral and Brain Sciences* 19 (4): 642–43.

Piattelli-Palmarini, M. 1989. "Evolution, Selection and Cognition: From 'Learning' to Parameter Setting in Biology and the Study of Language." *Cognition* 31:1–44.

——. 2008. *Le scienze cognitive classiche: Un panorama*. Ed. N. Canessa and A. Gorini. Turin: Einaudi.

Pinborg, J. 1982. "Speculative Grammar." In *The Cambridge History of Later Medieval Philosophy: From the Rediscovery of Aristotle to the Disintegration of Scholasticism 1100–1600*, ed. N. Kretzmann, A. Kenny, and J. Pinborg, 254–70. Cambridge: Cambridge University Press.

Reichenbach, H. 1977. *The Philosophy of Space and Time*. New York: Dover.

Rizzi, L. 1990. *Relativized Minimality*. Cambridge, Mass.: MIT Press.

——. 2009. "The Discovery of Language Invariance and Variation, and Its Relevance for the Cognitive Sciences." *Behavioral and Brain Sciences* 32:467–68.

Russell, B. 1945. *A History of Western Philosophy*. London: George Allen and Unwin.

Russell, J. 2004. *What Is Language Development: Rationalist, Empiricist, and Pragmatist Approaches to the Acquisition of Syntax*. Oxford: Oxford University Press.

Schrödinger, E. 1944. *What Is Life?*. Cambridge: Cambridge University Press.

Tattersal, I. 2012. *Masters of the Planet: The Search for Our Human Origins*. London: Palgrave Macmillan.

Terrace, H.-S., L.-A. Petitto, R.-J. Sanders, and T.-G. Bever. 1979. "Can an Ape Create a Sentence?" *Science* 206 (4421): 891–902.

Tettamanti, M., H. Alkadhi, A. Moro, D. Perani, S. Kollias, and D. Weniger. 2002. "Neural Correlates for the Acquisition of Natural Language Syntax." *NeuroImage* 17:700–9.

Tettamanti, M., R. Manenti, P. Della Rosa, A. Falini, D. Perani, S. Cappa, and A. Moro. 2008a. "Negation in the Brain: Modulating Action Representations." *NeuroImage* 43 (2): 358–67.

Tettamanti, M., and A. Moro. 2012. "Can Syntax Appear in a Mirror (System)?" *Cortex: Special Issue on Language and Motor Systems Cortex* 48 (7): 923–35.

Tettamanti, M., I. Rotondi, D. Perani, G. Scotti, F. Fazio, S. F. Cappa, and A. Moro. 2008b. "Syntax Without Language: Neurobiological Evidence for Cross-Domain Syntactic Computations." *Cortex* 45 (7): 825–38.

Trautteur, G. 2002. "Undici tesi sulla scienza cognitive." *Adelphiana* 1:71–96.

Turing, A. M. 1950. "Computing Machinery and Intelligence." *Mind* 59:433–60.

Veca, S. 2011. *L'idea di incompletezza: Quattro lezioni*. Milan: Feltrinelli.

Westfall, R. 1983. *Never at Rest*. Cambridge: Cambridge University Press.

Wilson, R., and F. Keil. 1999. *The MIT Encyclopedia of the Cognitive Sciences*. Cambridge, Mass.: MIT Press.

Zellini, P. 2010. *Logos e numero*. Milan: Adelphi.